Shakespeare for the Seeker

Volume 1

Wes Jamroz

Troubadour Publications

SHAKESPEARE FOR THE SEEKER

Volume 1

This is a revised edition of the previously published booklets:

"The Developmental Cycle in the History Plays" (2008)
"First Encounters" (2008)
"Previous Developmental Cycle" (2009)
"Reformation" (2009)

Editing:	*David Sereda, Dominique Hugon*
Cover design:	*Sandra Viscuso*
Illustrations:	*Jeff Burgess*

P.O. Box # 76, Station N.D.G.
Montreal, Quebec
Canada
H4A 3P6
TroubadourPubs@aol.com
http://www.troubadourpublications

ISBN: 978-0-9869673-1-3

Evolutionary branches in Shakespeare's plays

Date	Play	Time setting	Branch
1602	Troilus and Cressida	13th century BC	Starting point
1608	Pericles, Prince of Tyre	From 10th century BC (est.) to 12th century	Modern cycle
1608	Coriolanus	5th century BC	Roman
1599	Julius Caesar	44 BC	Roman
1606	Antony and Cleopatra	33 - 30 BC	Roman
1594	Titus Andronicus	4th century	Roman
1605	King Lear	10th century BC (est.)	Celtic
1610	Cymbeline	1st century, and 9th century, and 16th century	Celtic
1605	Macbeth	11th century	Celtic
1607	Timon of Athens	4th century	Bohemian
1593	The Comedy of Errors	9th century	Bohemian
1611	The Winter's Tale	13th century	Bohemian
1601	Twelfth Night	15th century	Bohemian
1604	Measure for Measure	16th century	Bohemian
1601	Hamlet	16th century	Bohemian
1596	King John	1199 - 1216	English
1595	Richard II	1377 - 1399	English
1598	Henry IV (part 1, 2)	1399 - 1413	English
1599	Henry V	1413 - 1422	English
1591	Henry VI (part 1, 2, 3)	1422 - 1471	English
1592	Richard III	1483 - 1485	English
1613	Henry VIII	1509 - 1533	English
1602	All's Well That Ends Well	13th and 16th century	French
1599	As You Like It	15th century	French
1595	Love's Labour's Lost	16th century	French
1604	Othello	14th century	Italian
1599	Much Ado About Nothing	15th century	Italian
1597	The Merchant of Venice	16th century	Italian
1594	The Taming of the Shrew	16th century	Italian
1595	Romeo and Juliet	16th century	Italian
1594	Two Gentlemen of Verona	16th century	Italian
1599	The Merry Wives of Windsor	17th century	New cycle
1611	The Tempest	17th century	New cycle
1595	A Midsummer Night's Dream	17th century	Conclusion

Table of Contents

CHAPTER 1

Evolutionary Cycle in the History Plays

Wes Jamroz

Introduction

A new phase of spiritual teaching was initiated in Europe in the early 60s. This new phase was dictated by the needs of the time, place and people there. A group of initiates was formed under the direction of a guide. One of their tasks was to mount a stage performance of Shakespeare's "Henry V". The performance was staged in a private atelier in Montparnasse, in Paris. It lasted nearly all day. Those who were acting were also the audience. The question may be asked: how is "Henry V" related to spiritual teaching?

An answer to the above question may be found in Shakespeare's History Plays.

Historical background

The History Plays written by Shakespeare are generally thought of as a distinct type as they differ somewhat in tone, form and focus from his other plays which are usually classified as comedies and tragedies. The History Plays were set in late medieval England. They include ten plays: "King John", "Richard II", "Henry IV" (parts 1 and 2), "Henry V", "Henry VI" (parts 1, 2 and 3), "Richard III", and "Henry VIII".

These plays dramatize several generations of medieval power struggles, starting with the reign of King John (1199) until the reign of Henry VIII and the birth of Elizabeth I (1533). This period includes the Hundred Years War with France and the Wars of the Roses. The Hundred Years War was a conflict between France and England. It lasted 116 years, from 1337 to 1453. The war was fought primarily over claims by the English kings to the French throne.

The Wars of the Roses (1455–1487) were a series of civil conflicts fought over the throne of England between supporters of the House of Lancaster and the House of York. Both houses were branches of the Plantagenet royal house, tracing their descent to Geoffrey the Fair, Duke of Anjou. This conflict was called "the Wars of the Roses" after the symbols of each house, the red rose of Lancaster and the white rose of York. The conflict was not laid to rest until, as Shakespeare describes it at the end of "Richard III", a son of the House of Lancaster marries a daughter of the House of York, and, as Henry VII, founds the Tudor dynasty.

Henry VIII and his daughter Elizabeth I were monarchs belonging to the Tudor dynasty.

Manifest faculties

One of the functions of spiritual teaching is to project into the world of ordinary senses examples that parallel events from a higher realm. Shakespeare's plays are an example of such a projection.

The whole of the universe presents an integrated pattern and all created things are linked together. The universe is arranged according to a universal design that is based upon the principle of hierarchy. This hierarchy is very often compared to the patterns observed among plants, animals, and heavenly bodies. For example, the rose to the flowers bears the same relation as the oak to the trees, or the honeybee to the insects, or the eagle to the birds, or the lion to the beasts, or the sun to other heavenly bodies. Among men a king is above his subjects. However, the notion of a "king" is used in a different context than that ordinarily applied. Namely, a spiritually developed man is superior to other men. Developed man is just as much a separate species among the various kinds of men, as man is a separate species within other creatures. It is in this context that Shakespeare's "king" may be understood. This is why Shakespeare often compares a reigning king to a lion, an eagle, or the sun. The "king", in this symbolic language, represents a developed aspect of a human being, while members of the royal court symbolize other aspects of this being. These various aspects, in turn, are representation of the various faculties of a human being.

The human inner being consists of three centres or manifest faculties: self, heart, and intellect. Survival, as well as the desire for and the pursuit of pleasure, ambitions, self-importance and greed - all these are the attributes of the self faculty. Entertaining feelings of love and hatred, showing bravery or cowardice, forming an intention and carrying out a particular action - these are the characteristics of the heart faculty. Understanding and knowledge, the capacity to perceive, to recollect the things of the past and plan for the things of the future - these are the qualities that are attributed to the intellect faculty. The sum-total of the relationships between these three faculties forms an individual's character and his personality.

The position of the faculties within the human body is precisely determined. The self faculty permeates the whole body, but is firmly rooted in the liver; the heart faculty is present throughout the whole body, but it is firmly rooted in the physical heart; and the intellect faculty also pervades the entire body, but it is firmly rooted in the brain.

The behaviour of an ordinary human being is driven by his survival needs and by the desires of his self faculty. Such undeveloped behaviour undermines and contaminates the proper functioning of the other manifest faculties. In such an underdeveloped stage a human being is not able to make full use of life; it may be said that the ordinary man is asleep. Man may be "awakened" by coming into contact with an impulse of evolutionary energy. In this way the manifest faculties may be reformed and purified.

The reformation of the manifest faculties is a two-step process. The first step is achieved when the intellect faculty controls the other faculties, the heart and the self. The second step requires that the being should be reformed in such a way that the intellect should control the heart, and the heart should rule over the self; from the combination of these two forms of control, higher developmental stages may result.

The intellect and the heart faculties are not homogenous. They consist of a multi-layered inner structure. This inner structure may be unfolded, layer-by-layer, during the purification process. Therefore, the purification is also a multi-step process. At each step of the purification a subtler layer of the intellect or the heart may be activated. These more subtle layers are known as special or inner faculties. Sometimes the number "ninety nine" is used to denote these innumerable subtle layers. This symbolic representation indicates that one has to experience "ninety nine" purifying states to activate the inner faculties. Consequently, the number "one hundred" indicates the completion of the purification.

The reformation and the purification may be realized by exposure to a spectrum of evolutionary energies. First, the evolutionary energy is delivered to the brain. Then it is carried along the veins to the heart and subsequently to the liver, gradually rarefying the manifest faculties. Sir John Falstaff in "Henry IV" gives a compelling description of this process when he talks about the effect of wine (sherris) on "this little kingdom":

> "A good sherris sack hath a two-fold
> operation in it. It ascends me into the brain;
> dries me there all the foolish and dull and curdy
> vapours which environ it; makes it apprehensive,
> quick, forgetive, full of nimble fiery and
> delectable shapes, which, delivered o'er to the
> voice, the tongue, which is the birth, becomes
> excellent wit. The second property of your

excellent sherris is, the warming of the blood;
which, before cold and settled, left the liver
white and pale, which is the badge of pusillanimity
and cowardice; but the sherris warms it and makes
it course from the inwards to the parts extreme:
it illumineth the face, which as a beacon gives
warning to all the rest of this little kingdom,
man, to arm; and then the vital commoners and
inland petty spirits muster me all to their captain,
the heart, who, great and puffed up with this
retinue, doth any deed of courage; and this valour
comes of sherris."

If we assume that the drinking of sherris symbolically illustrates the effect of the exposure of the brain, the heart, and the liver to evolutionary energy, then it becomes obvious that Falstaff's description parallels the evolutionary process. It is the process that may make a gloomy one joyful, a coward brave, and an ignoramus clever.

It should be emphasized that in the History Plays, the characters representing the kings do not always represent the reformed or the purified aspects of the faculties. Very often, particularly at the initial stages of the process, the king represents the dominant or the leading aspect of a being. Therefore, it is sometimes difficult to determine which characters represent the developed aspects of the being. Sometimes the developed aspects may shift from one character to others. And this is the reason for so many ambiguous reactions and behaviour of the various characters in the plays. All these situations are used to illustrate the complexities of the evolutionary process.

Evolutionary cycle

The History Plays describe a cycle of the evolutionary process of a human being. This being is called England. In this case, England represents both an individual human being and a fraction of medieval Western European society. In the case of an individual, such a cycle covers the lifespan of an adult person. In the case of a historical culture, such a cycle may require several centuries for its completion.

The process is fuelled by the presence of evolutionary energies. These energies have a wave-like form, i.e., they operate according to a certain predetermined pattern. Their occurrence at a given place, situation and time is predictable to a degree. Their wave-like form is characterized by a crest that is followed by a trough. Because of the wave-like nature of these energies, an initiate goes through a number of stages and states. The full evolutionary cycle, from the initiation to its completion, may be divided into seven stages. For example, the stages of the lowest cycle of the evolutionary spiral may be described as:

1. Initiation ("King John")
2. Preliminary realization ("Richard II")
3. Partial reformation ("Henry IV")
4. Dawn of perfection ("Henry V")
5. Inception of purification ("Henry VI")
6. Completion of purification ("Richard III")
7. Activation of permanent consciousness ("Henry VIII")

The term "stage" refers to an attribute, which the individual may acquire as the result of his exposure to evolutionary energy and which enables him to continue and complete the process. The transformation from one stage to the next is associated with experiences that may be termed "death" and "rebirth". These transformations are the origin of such phrases as "man must die before he dies" or that "man must be born again". In the plays the reigning king represents the leading characteristic of a given stage. However, each stage is determined by the presence and composition of all aspects of the being. Various modes of their appearance, i.e., their uniformity, degree of negativity, ability to act together, depth of intuitive understanding, etc., characterize each stage. These various modes of appearance are termed "states". Hence the "stage" is regarded as an acquisition, while "states" refer to actual products of the stage. It should be pointed out that a stage arises in one individual in one form, and in a different form in someone else. Therefore, there is a whole range of states associated with each stage.

The first stage marks the initiation of a disciple. A disciple is exposed to an impulse of evolutionary energy.

The second stage is the beginning of mental integration, when the mind is becoming capable of operating on a higher level than was its previous futile custom. The individual starts to realize that he, like all underdeveloped men, has a multiple and changing personality.

The third stage is marked by the dawn of self-awareness.

At the fourth stage, the individual is capable of experiencing the first taste of the manifestation of the reformed faculties. This is experienced by the brief appearance of new ranges of capacities that are beyond ordinary powers.

This in turn is followed by the fifth stage that is characterized by the appearance of destructive elements that until that time were dormant. A temporary vanishing of the previously experienced states marks this stage. Instead, the individual experiences distress and doubts.

At the sixth stage the destructive aspects are manifested in their fullest strength. Now, because these destructive aspects have been fully exposed, it is possible to identify and then diminish them. In other words, this is the cleansing effect. Afterwards, the individual is ready to absorb evolutionary energy in a much more effective manner.

The evolutionary cycle is completed when the individual achieves the capacity of objective understanding. The individual acquires a new organ of perception that allows him to operate in accordance with the universal design. Now he may enter onto the next cycle of the evolutionary spiral, which is a notch higher than the previous one.

In the case of the History Plays, the degree of harmony between various aspects of the being, their ability to act together, and their depth of intuitive understanding increases gradually from play to play. It is this degree of the overall unity of these various aspects that marks the gradual progress. This progress is manifested, among other things, by the ability of the king to perceive the depth of his role and his responsibility.

Shakespeare uses the History Plays to illustrate the various stages of the cycle. It is a very interesting example, because it allows to see the evolutionary process as applied to an individual human being as well as to an actual historical culture that had tangible impact on progress in Western Europe.

Initiation ("King John")

At the beginning of the process there must be a contact with evolutionary energy. A person, a group of people, a country, or a culture acquires an evolutionary impulse and then gradually integrates it within itself. At that moment the being receives an impression, just as wax receives the impression of the signet ring. This impression allows for holding and digesting the initial impulse. This stage of the process is called initiation and it may be compared to organic engrafting.

The initiation may be realized in many ways. For example, a group of initiates may form an association that shall enable them to carry on their developmental work. Such work has usually three parts. Firstly, the individual himself or herself must live up to certain personal standards and they might choose, for example, the medieval ideal of chivalry as their format. This, in turn, would give them the opportunity of forming a visible elite. The existence and appearance of such an elite would fulfill the second function by their impact upon humanity in general. The third element would be related to their reverence for the guide who leads the community. The group would adopt certain colours as their symbols to indicate their developmental objectives. For example, if their prime objective were the reformation of the manifest faculties, then most probably for their colour symbols they would adopt gold and blue. These colours symbolize the sun in the blue sky. The clear unclouded blue sky symbolizes the balanced mind, within which it is possible to see the gold, i.e., to experience true nobility in its first manifestation. This particular colour code was the origin of the "blue blooded nobility", the term that indicated the existence of spiritually developed men among ordinary humanity.

The basic unit of such a group would be called a circle that could be symbolized, for example, by a garter.

There is a historical record of such an initiatory group that has been used by Shakespeare in the History Plays. The group has been known as the Order of the Garter. The Order of the Garter was created in 1348. It was inspired by King Edward III. However, it is important to realize that the Order of the Garter was the result of much earlier events that formed the origin of its conception. Namely, it was related to activities associated with the Plantagenet dynasty.

The whole Plantagenet dynasty was deeply involved in activities that were responsible, among other things, for the creation of chivalric orders in Europe. Geoffrey the Fair, Duke of Anjou (1113 - 1151) adopted as his family emblem the broom plant (*planta genista*), hence the Plantagenets. The broom indicates a "forceful occasion". The forceful occasion means the "right time, right people, and right place". In other words, a person displaying a broom plant signals that he, or she, is capable of recognizing such an occasion and knows how to use it for developmental purposes.

The members of the Order of the Garter were divided into two circles of thirteen each, one under Edward III and the other under his eldest son, the Black Prince. Its colours were blue and gold. Its aims were overtly chivalric. Its patron saint was St. George. They chose as their slogan a salutation to the cupbearer, i.e., their spiritual guide. This salutation, in its original language, sounded very similar to the French "*Honi soit qui mal y pense*". Later on this sound has been adopted as its literary English translation, i.e., "Dishonored be he who thinks evil of it". Shakespeare discreetly indicates the corruption of this slogan by paraphrasing it into "tell truth and shame the devil". It is Hotspur in "Henry IV", one of the historical Knights of the Order of the Garter, who uses this phrase when he talks to Glendower:

"And I can teach thee, coz, to shame the devil
By telling truth: tell truth and shame the devil.
If thou have power to raise him, bring him hither,
And I'll be sworn I have power to shame him hence.
O, while you live, tell truth and shame the devil!"

There is a reference to the patron saint of the Order of the Garter
when Henry V rallies his troops during the siege on Harfleur:

"Follow your spirit, and upon this charge
Cry 'God for Harry, England, and Saint George!' "

Another reference to the Order of the Garter is given when Talbot,
another historical Knight of the Order of the Garter that appears
in the History Plays, is taking away the garter from Fastolfe who
did run cowardly away from the battle of Patay ("Henry VI"):

"I vow'd, base knight, when I did meet thee next,
To tear the garter from thy craven's leg."

As the result of the initiation, the being acquires a new aspect
within itself. At the beginning of the process this aspect could be
described as an alien or as a bastard if one would like to draw a
parallel to social or family structure. Such a bastardized aspect
would be recognized and accepted only by some more balanced
elements of the being. At the initial stage, however, the being
would not be ready to allow a bastard to play a leading role.
Therefore, this aspect would operate in the background, discreetly
guiding the being.

It is the Bastard, a character from "King John", who plays such a
role. It is the Bastard who represents the link to the original
evolutionary impulse. Shakespeare indicates that the Bastard in
"King John" is linked to the historical figure of Richard I:

"King Richard Coeur-de-lion was thy father."

At this point it should be recalled that the king Richard I was
grandson of Geoffrey of Anjou. Richard I was the famous Coeur-
de-lion (Lionheart). This name contains the initiatory words

"heart" and "lion". The "heart" refers to the purified (spiritual) heart faculty. The "lion" means a "man of the way", that is an aspirant on the way to higher development. Richard's nickname is thus an announcement, to those who understand, that he has been initiated.

Shakespeare gives an example of the Bastard's chivalric conduct in the episode of the battle of Angers. Philip, King of France, and his forces prepare to attack the English-held town of Angers unless its citizens swear allegiance to Arthur. Arthur legally should have been the king of England. However, Richard the Lionheart, who was the previous king, appointed more capable John as his successor. King John and his armies also arrive at Angers. Both kings ask Angers' citizens whom they recognize as their king. The citizens shrewdly reply that they support the rightful king. Philip' and John's armies go to war, but are so equally matched that neither side wins. The citizens of Angers still won't decide between them. Then the Bastard resolves the situation by suggesting that the English and French armies unite to conquer the disobedient town of Angers, and fight each other later. They agree and prepare to attack. At this point, the citizens of Angers suggest an alternative and the impasse is resolved.

The Bastard becomes the most compelling character in the play. He is unswervingly loyal to the king. At the same time he is not afraid to point out mistakes made by the king. For example, he denounces deals made between King John and the King of France, and between King John and the Pope. He criticizes the royal desire for riches and self-interest. In other words, the Bastard discreetly guides the being of England.

At the end of the play King John dies. The Bastard and the lords swear allegiance to John's son – Prince Henry. Henry becomes King Henry III and the lords swear allegiance to him over his father's dead body. The Bastard makes the final speech of the play in which he cheers on the unconquerable force of England:

> "This England never did, nor never shall,
> Lie at the proud foot of a conqueror,
> But when it first did help to wound itself."

The Bastard confirms England's potential for development, but he indicates that this being has to be reformed first before it can experience its higher modes of functioning. The being of England, although initiated and charged with the impulse of evolutionary energy, has to go through several stages.

Incidentally, the period corresponding to the reign of King John was marked in history by the issue of the *Magna Carta*, the most significant document that initiated the West into a process that led to the rule of constitutional law. The *Magna Carta* is considered one of the most important legal documents in the history of western democracy.

Preliminary realization ("Richard II")

An initiatory impulse allows a being to start to realize its evolutionary possibilities, although at this stage, the being still treats such a possibility as a sort of secondary priority. Nevertheless, the presence of such an initiatory impulse creates a certain constructive tension within the being. Its developmental effect may be fully realized only after recognition of the limitations that are imposed by worldly ambitions and wants. Signs of such recognition are indicated by King Richard II in his soliloquy:

> "I'll give my jewels for a set of beads,
> My gorgeous palace for a hermitage,
> My gay apparel for an almsman's gown,
> My figured goblets for a dish of wood,
> My sceptre for a palmer's walking staff,
> My subjects for a pair of carved saints
> And my large kingdom for a little grave,
> A little little grave, an obscure grave."

Richard is the main character of the second play of the History Plays. It should be noted that King Richard II was the first among the kings of England who was initiated into the Order of the Garter. Another main historical character of this play is John of Gaunt who was also a Knight of the Order of the Garter.

Richard, who ascended to the throne as a young man, is a regal and stately figure, but he is wasteful in his spending habits, unwise in his choice of counsellors and detached from his country and its people. He spends too much of his time pursuing the latest fashions, spending money, and raising taxes to fund his pet wars in Ireland and elsewhere. When he begins to rent out parcels of English land to certain wealthy noblemen in order to raise funds for one of his wars, and when he seizes the lands and money of a recently deceased and much respected uncle to help fill his coffers, both the noblemen and the commoners decide that Richard has gone too far.

Richard has a cousin, named Henry Bolingbroke, who is a great favourite among the English commoners. Henry is the son of Richard's uncle, John of Gaunt. Henry is far more pragmatic and capable than Richard.

Early in the play, Richard exiles Henry from England for six years due to an unresolved dispute over an earlier political murder. The dead uncle whose lands Richard seizes was John of Gaunt. When Henry learns that Richard has stolen what should have been his inheritance, he assembles an army and invades England. The commoners, fond of Henry and angry at Richard's mismanagement of the country, welcome his invasion and join his forces. One by one, Richard's allies desert him and defect to Henry's side. There is never an actual battle; instead, Henry peacefully takes Richard prisoner. Richard is imprisoned in a remote castle. Henry is crowned as King Henry IV. Later on, an assassin, who follows Henry's ambivalent wish, murders Richard.

As in the other plays, the king, members of his family and his courtiers represent various aspects of the manifest faculties of the being of England. Since the initiation there is always one aspect that provides a link to the initial evolutionary impulse. Such aspects form an internal transmission chain. At the same time, there are a few individuals among those representing the various aspects of the intellectual faculty who are aware of the higher purpose of this being. However, such awareness takes the form of brief moments that appear only infrequently. Very often these flashes of realization seem to be confusing and imprecise. These happen in situations when the king's actions are questionable or go against ordinary moral, religious, or social norms. It seems that there is an awareness, at least among some of the courtiers, of the concept of the "king", his role and his function. Although at this stage of the development, they do not have the capacity, as yet, to recognize the righteous "king". Therefore, they are confused because they are using artificial means to determine who the king is or who should be recognized as the king. At this stage of development, England has not yet experienced the taste of perfected states. Therefore, the understanding and behaviour of the various aspects of this being are still driven by theoretical and conceptual beliefs.

For example, John of Gaunt refuses to take action against King Richard. His reasoning is based on his conceptual belief that God divinely appoints the king of the nation. He refuses to attack the murderers of his brother, because the person who is most to blame for the murder is King Richard himself. Gaunt refuses to raise arms against the king, not out of loyalty to him as a relative, nor out of fear for the power of the king, but rather because he believes, as do many of the play's other characters, that the king of a nation was appointed by Heaven, and that an act of rebellion against the king would therefore be blasphemous. If Richard has caused Gaunt's brother's death, then Heaven must revenge it; because Richard is the Lord's substitute, and, as Gaunt says:

"I may never lift
An angry arm against His minister."

As has been mentioned earlier, at this stage of the development, the individual starts to realize that he, like all underdeveloped persons, has a multiple and changing personality. This is quite remarkably illustrated in Richard's soliloquy while he is in prison. Richard indicates to the audience that his own thoughts could be represented as various people:

"My brain I'll prove the female to my soul,
My soul the father; and these two beget
A generation of still-breeding thoughts,
And these same thoughts people this little world."

Richard's language may seem to be obscure unless the readers realize that Shakespeare describes a certain stage of the evolutionary process. Namely, Richard's realization about his multiple and changing personality marks the arrival of England on the second stage of the cycle.

Partial reformation ("Henry IV")

The awareness of multiple and changing personalities induces a constructive mental action that may lead to the reformation of some of the leading tendencies of the being. Shakespeare illustrates this stage of the process in "Henry IV".

The play is set in the first years of the 15th century. At that time England is in the middle of a civil war. Powerful rebels have assembled against King Henry IV in an attempt to overthrow him. King Henry has recently become very ill because of his anxiety over the war, his implication in the death of King Richard, and the misbehaviour of his eldest son, Prince Henry. In the meantime the rebel leaders gather their forces to battle the king.

The play includes dialogues and monologues that are like intellectual duels of opposing arguments. There are no winning arguments as all of them are intellectually convincing.

According to spiritual teaching's motto, "things outwardly opposed may inwardly be working together", such intellectual duels of opposite arguments serve the same purpose: they indicate the limitation of the ordinary and underdeveloped intellect. For it is said that any attempt to understand the evolutionary process by application of intellection may be compared to barbarism, because a barbarian is one whose perceptions are so insensitive that he thinks that he can understand by thinking or feeling something which can be perceived only through development and constant application to the striving towards divine perfection. The awareness of such limitation triggers a constructive mental action that may lead to the reformation of the intellect faculty.

As an example, here is Sir John Falstaff's monologue on honour:

"Can honour set to a leg? no: or
an arm? no: or take away the grief of a wound? no.
Honour hath no skill in surgery, then? no. What is
honour? a word. What is in that word honour?
what is that honour? air. A trim reckoning! Who
hath it? he that died o' Wednesday. Doth he feel
it? no. Doth he hear it? no. 'Tis insensible, then.
Yea, to the dead. But will it not live with the
living? no. Why? detraction will not suffer it.
Therefore I'll none of it. Honour is a mere
scutcheon: and so ends my catechism."

Later on we will see how Falstaff's understanding differs from that of Henry V's explanation of honour. Falstaff's way of thinking is an example of the working of an atrophied intellect. His way of thinking lacks deeper perception. This lack of perception is a barrier that, later on, will exclude Falstaff from Henry V's companionship.

There are many comments in "Henry IV" that point towards various teaching techniques that may be employed at this stage of development. For example, here is Worcester's lesson to Hotspur on proper conduct:

"In faith, my lord, you are too wilful-blame;
And since your coming hither have done enough
To put him quite beside his patience.
You must needs learn, lord, to amend this fault:
Though sometimes it show greatness, courage, blood,
And that's the dearest grace it renders you,
Yet oftentimes it doth present harsh rage,
Defect of manners, want of government,
Pride, haughtiness, opinion and disdain."

Or the Archbishop's comments on self-observation that may allow one to recognize the way in which the ordinary self faculty operates. In this case the operation of the self faculty is compared to the behaviour of the masses ("the commonwealth"):

"The commonwealth is sick of their own choice;
Their over-greedy love hath surfeited:
An habitation giddy and unsure
Hath he that buildeth on the vulgar heart.
O thou fond many, with what loud applause
Didst thou beat heaven with blessing Bolingbroke,
Before he was what thou wouldst have him be!
And being now trimm'd in thine own desires,
Thou, beastly feeder, art so full of him,
That thou provokest thyself to cast him up.
So, so, thou common dog, didst thou disgorge
Thy glutton bosom of the royal Richard;
And now thou wouldst eat thy dead vomit up,
And howl'st to find it. What trust is in these times?
They that, when Richard lived, would have him die,
Are now become enamour'd on his grave."

Throughout the play Henry retains his tight, tenuous hold on the throne, and he never loses his majesty. Henry remains stern, aloof, and resolute, but he is no longer the force of nature he appears to be in "Richard II". At the same time, however, he becomes reflective about his role and his responsibilities. His gradual awakening is marked by his lack of sleep:

"How many thousand of my poorest subjects
Are at this hour asleep! O sleep, O gentle sleep,
Nature's soft nurse, how have I frighted thee,
That thou no more wilt weigh my eyelids down
And steep my senses in forgetfulness?
Why rather, sleep, liest thou in smoky cribs,
Upon uneasy pallets stretching thee
And hush'd with buzzing night-flies to thy slumber,
Than in the perfumed chambers of the great,
Under the canopies of costly state,
And lull'd with sound of sweetest melody?
O thou dull god, why liest thou with the vile
In loathsome beds, and leavest the kingly couch
A watch-case or a common 'larum-bell?
Wilt thou upon the high and giddy mast

Seal up the ship-boy's eyes, and rock his brains
In cradle of the rude imperious surge
And in the visitation of the winds,
Who take the ruffian billows by the top,
Curling their monstrous heads and hanging them
With deafening clamour in the slippery clouds,
That, with the hurly, death itself awakes?
Canst thou, O partial sleep, give thy repose
To the wet sea-boy in an hour so rude,
And in the calmest and most stillest night,
With all appliances and means to boot,
Deny it to a king? Then happy low, lie down!
Uneasy lies the head that wears a crown."

The above monologue marks the third stage of the cycle. The being experiences the dawn of self-awareness.

At the end of the play there are some indications that new forces are starting to manifest themselves. For example, Henry's vicious enemy Hotspur starts to realize that somehow his luck disappears. This is illustrated by the sudden sickness of Hotspur's father:

"Sick now! droop now! this sickness doth infect
The very life-blood of our enterprise;
'Tis catching hither, even to our camp.
He writes me here, that inward sickness
And that his friends by deputation could not
So soon be drawn, nor did he think it meet
To lay so dangerous and dear a trust
On any soul removed but on his own.
Yet doth he give us bold advertisement,
That with our small conjunction we should on,
To see how fortune is disposed to us;
For, as he writes, there is no quailing now.
Because the king is certainly possess'd
Of all our purposes."

These invisible forces are not clearly defined yet. Nevertheless, they indicate the arrival of England at the next stage of the process.

Dawn of perfection ("Henry V")

The next stage leads to the experience of the true taste of a higher level of being. England has reached the stage that corresponds to the correctly reformed being. Here it is how Canterbury uses the example of honeybees to describe this stage:

> "Therefore doth heaven divide
> The state of man in divers functions,
> Setting endeavour in continual motion;
> To which is fixed, as an aim or butt,
> Obedience: for so work the honey-bees,
> Creatures that by a rule in nature teach
> The act of order to a peopled kingdom.
> They have a king and officers of sorts;
> Where some, like magistrates, correct at home,
> Others, like merchants, venture trade abroad,
> Others, like soldiers, armed in their stings,
> Make boot upon the summer's velvet buds,
> Which pillage they with merry march bring home
> To the tent-royal of their emperor;
> Who, busied in his majesty, surveys
> The singing masons building roofs of gold,
> The civil citizens kneading up the honey,
> The poor mechanic porters crowding in
> Their heavy burdens at his narrow gate,
> The sad-eyed justice, with his surly hum,
> Delivering o'er to executors pale
> The lazy yawning drone. I this infer,
> That many things, having full reference
> To one consent, may work contrariously."

The leading character of the play is King Henry V. Henry, as a young man, spent most of his time in taverns on the seedy side of London, hanging around with vagrants and other shady characters. Here is how Warwick explained this behaviour of the young Prince:

> "My gracious lord, you look beyond him quite:
> The prince but studies his companions
> Like a strange tongue, wherein, to gain the language,

'Tis needful that the most immodest word
Be look'd upon and learn'd; which once attain'd,
Your highness knows, comes to no further use
But to be known and hated. So, like gross terms,
The prince will in the perfectness of time
Cast off his followers; and their memory
Shall as a pattern or a measure live,
By which his grace must mete the lives of others,
Turning past evils to advantages."

King Henry V represents the reformed intellect faculty. The above quote is the description of a part of his preparatory training. This training is followed by the activation of the reformed intellect faculty. Such transformation may be compared to the appearance of a new flower, or a new tree that has taken root in the garden and is showing its first buds. It is a sort of organic transmutation. Shakespeare has quite precisely described it the change that has been observed in the young Prince Henry at the moment of his father's death:

"The breath no sooner left his father's body,
But that his wildness, mortified in him,
Seem'd to die too; yea, at that very moment
Consideration, like an angel, came
And whipp'd the offending Adam out of him,
Leaving his body as a paradise,
To envelop and contain celestial spirits.
Never was such a sudden scholar made;
Never came reformation in a flood,
With such a heady currance, scouring faults
Nor never Hydra-headed wilfulness
So soon did lose his seat and all at once
As in this king."

It should be emphasized that it was the Bastard in "King John" who provided the seed of this new tree.

The transformation of young Henry affected his knowledge of theological matters, domestic policy, war strategy, and political topics. The rebirth of Henry has been a puzzle to many, because the young Prince used to spend a lot of time drinking with uneducated, crude and superficial companions. He used to get drunk, seeking out entertainment, seemingly with no interest at all in learning or contemplation.

However, this transformation requires that Henry leaves behind his former companions, including Sir John Falstaff. Falstaff, back in those wild days, had been his closest friend and mentor. He had been a jovial and frequently drunken old knight. Now Falstaff's heart is broken because Henry, after becoming king, has cut off his ties with him. This is what Henry explained to Falstaff:

> "I know thee not, old man: fall to thy prayers;
> How ill white hairs become a fool and jester!
> I have long dream'd of such a kind of man,
> So surfeit-swell'd, so old and so profane;
> But, being awaked, I do despise my dream.
> Make less thy body hence, and more thy grace;
> Leave gormandizing; know the grave doth gape
> For thee thrice wider than for other men.
> Reply not to me with a fool-born jest:
> Presume not that I am the thing I was;
> For God doth know, so shall the world perceive,
> That I have turn'd away my former self;
> So will I those that kept me company.
> When thou dost hear I am as I have been,
> Approach me, and thou shalt be as thou wast,
> The tutor and the feeder of my riots:
> Till then, I banish thee, on pain of death,
> As I have done the rest of my misleaders,
> Not to come near our person by ten mile.
> For competence of life I will allow you,
> That lack of means enforce you not to evil:
> And, as we hear you do reform yourselves,
> We will, according to your strengths and qualities,
> Give you advancement. Be it your charge, my lord,
> To see perform'd the tenor of our word. Set on."

Henry has to leave his former companions behind because they have not been able to perceive and understand the transformation that has taken place. Therefore, they have not been able to harmonize themselves with this new phase of Henry's function and his mission.

Henry's mission is symbolically described as the Battle for France. It may help to comprehend the described process if we remember that Henry represents the reformed intellect faculty, while France in the History Plays symbolizes the underdeveloped and unruly heart faculty. As has been mentioned previously, the required remedy is that the reformed intellect should control the heart. This mission may also be viewed from the historical perspective. Namely, it may be presumed that the Battle for France was to reinstate a passive, recessive feminine element into the stream of European life. It has been suggested that this element was probably defective in the entire history of the West.

Henry lays claim to certain parts of France based on his distant roots in the French royal family and on a very technical interpretation of ancient land laws. When the Prince of France sends Henry an insulting message in response to these claims, Henry decides to invade France. Supported by the English noblemen and clergy, Henry gathers his troops for war.

The climax of the war comes at the famous Battle of Agincourt[1], at which the English are outnumbered by the French five to one. The night before the battle, King Henry disguises himself as a common soldier and talks to the soldiers in his camp, to reaffirm who they are and what they think. During that night Michael Williams, a common soldier, challenges the king's cause for the war:

> "But if the cause be not good, the king himself hath
> a heavy reckoning to make, when all those legs and
> arms and heads, chopped off in battle, shall join
> together at the latter day and cry all 'We died at
> such a place;' some swearing, some crying for a
> surgeon, some upon their wives left poor behind

[1] This is no coincidence that, geographically, Agincourt is located in the vicinity of the region of Arden, where the concluding scene of "As You Like It" takes place. At that time a spiritual heart was activated within the French branch of the modern evolutionary cycle (see Volume 2, Chapter 5).

them, some upon the debts they owe, some upon their children rawly left. I am afeard there are few die well that die in a battle; for how can they charitably dispose of any thing, when blood is their argument? Now, if these men do not die well, it will be a black matter for the king that led them to it; whom to disobey were against all proportion of subjection."

Henry delivers his reply that touches on some aspects of universal justice and destiny:

"So, if a son that is by his father sent about merchandise do sinfully miscarry upon the sea, the imputation of his wickedness by your rule, should be imposed upon his father that sent him: or if a servant, under his master's command transporting a sum of money, be assailed by robbers and die in many irreconciled iniquities, you may call the business of the master the author of the servant's damnation: but this is not so: the king is not bound to answer the particular endings of his soldiers, the father of his son, nor the master of his servant; for they purpose not their death, when they purpose their services. Besides, there is no king, be his cause never so spotless, if it come to the arbitrement of swords, can try it out with all unspotted soldiers: some peradventure have on them the guilt of premeditated and contrived murder; some, of beguiling virgins with the broken seals of perjury; some, making the wars their bulwark, that have before gored the gentle bosom of peace with pillage and robbery. Now, if these men have defeated the law and outrun native punishment, though they can outstrip men, they have no wings to fly from God: war is his beadle, war is vengeance; so that here men are punished for before-breach of the king's laws in now the king's quarrel: where they feared the death, they have borne life away; and where they

would be safe, they perish: then if they die
unprovided, no more is the king guilty of their
damnation than he was before guilty of those
impieties for the which they are now visited.
Every subject's duty is the king's; but every
subject's soul is his own. Therefore should every
soldier in the wars do as every sick man in his bed,
wash every mote out of his conscience: and dying
so, death is to him advantage; or not dying, the
time was blessedly lost wherein such preparation
was gained: and in him that escapes, it were not
sin to think that, making God so free an offer, He
let him outlive that day to see His greatness and to
teach others how they should prepare."

Then the play follows with Henry's soliloquy in which he reveals
the grave responsibilities he feels on his shoulders, with every man
of England laying his soul, debts, wives, children, and sin on the
king's head. Henry's perception of his role and his responsibility is
much deeper and more precise than that experienced by King
John, Richard II, or Henry IV:

"Upon the king! let us our lives, our souls,
Our debts, our careful wives,
Our children and our sins lay on the king!
We must bear all. O hard condition,
Twin-born with greatness, subject to the breath
Of every fool, whose sense no more can feel
But his own wringing! What infinite heart's-ease
Must kings neglect, that private men enjoy!
And what have kings, that privates have not too,
Save ceremony, save general ceremony?"

Henry describes the lonely isolation of his state, which is combined
with the need to be eternally vigilant. The king's consolation does
not encompass worldly matters. There is nothing in this world that
may reward him for his efforts. Some may think that the king's
reward lies in pomp and ceremony, with its rich clothes, parades,
and self-aggrandizement. Henry would rather trade all that
ceremony for the peaceful sleep of the slave, who has no greater

concerns in his head than his stomach and who has no idea what watch the King keeps to discharge his responsibility.

When Henry gives his famous St. Crispin's Day speech about honour, he talks about evolutionary energy. Evolutionary energy exists as a positive commodity; it can be accumulated and stored. When the time is ripe, it can be released into the world. Shakespeare uses the term "honour" to describe this energy. If reading it in this context, his speech becomes quite compelling indeed:

> "I pray thee, wish not one man more.
> By Jove, I am not covetous for gold,
> Nor care I who doth feed upon my cost;
> It yearns me not if men my garments wear;
> Such outward things dwell not in my desires:
> But if it be a sin to covet honour,
> I am the most offending soul alive.
> No, faith, my coz, wish not a man from England:
> God's peace! I would not lose so great an honour
> As one man more, methinks, would share from me
> For the best hope I have. O, do not wish one more!
> Rather proclaim it, Westmoreland, through my host,
> That he which hath no stomach to this fight,
> Let him depart; his passport shall be made
> And crowns for convoy put into his purse:
> We would not die in that man's company
> That fears his fellowship to die with us.
> This day is called the feast of Crispian:
> He that outlives this day, and comes safe home,
> Will stand a tip-toe when the day is named,
> And rouse him at the name of Crispian."

Henry portrays evolutionary energy as a fixed amount of honour that will be divided among all the victors. There is no need for unfit soldiers. If there were unfit men, then there would be less honour available for each worthy man, i.e., it would not be possible for each of these chosen men to have access to a certain critical mass of honour that is required to fulfill the potential of this particular forceful occasion. Henry thus gives his soldiers freedom to make the choice to fight with him or go home. Those who choose to stay and fight with him will be granted nobility, they will become brothers, and they will be elevated to a higher level of being:

> "We few, we happy few, we band of brothers;
> For he to-day that sheds his blood with me
> Shall be my brother; be he ne'er so vile,
> This day shall gentle his condition:
> And gentlemen in England now a-bed
> Shall think themselves accursed they were not here,
> And hold their manhoods cheap whiles any speaks
> That fought with us upon Saint Crispin's day."

The Battle of Agincourt is used by Shakespeare to describe an example of the manifestation of a forceful occasion. Henry's troops are able to rout the French despite the fact that they are outnumbered five to one.

The final scene of the play presents the achievement of the ultimate goal of this particular developmental stage, the reformation of the manifest faculties. Henry compares his state to that of the sun that "shines bright and never changes". It is clear that in his description of himself to Catherine, Henry is not talking about an ordinary man:

> "And while thou livest, dear Kate, take a fellow of
> plain and uncoined constancy; for he perforce
> must do thee right, because he hath not the gift to
> woo in other places: for these fellows of infinite
> tongue, that can rhyme themselves into ladies'
> favours, they do always reason themselves out
> again. What! a speaker is but a prater; a rhyme is
> but a ballad. A good leg will fall; a straight back
> will stoop; a black beard will turn white; a curled
> pate will grow bald; a fair face will wither; a full
> eye will wax hollow: but a good heart, Kate, is the
> sun and the moon; or, rather, the sun, and not the
> moon; for it shines bright and never changes, but
> keeps his course truly. If thou would have such a

one, take me; and take me, take a soldier; take a
soldier, take a king."

This scene marks the moment when the reformed intellect faculty
is united with the heart faculty. This allows England to enter onto
the next stage of the cycle. It should be noted though, that it is the
leading aspect of the being, Henry himself, who achieves this
elevated state. The other aspects of this being are able to taste this
elevated state only indirectly. Therefore, the other aspects of this
being have a long way to go before they themselves reach such a
state. This stage may be considered as the second initiation of
England. In other words, these other aspects of the being will have
to start the process from the beginning and go all the way to the
end.

The breakthrough experienced by England at this stage serves
several purposes. Firstly, it exposes the being to the taste of an
experience that is beyond the ordinary emotions and intellect. The
joy of such an experience increases the being's inner hunger
towards a higher level of fulfillment. Secondly, such an experience
starts the process of polarization between constructive and
destructive aspects of the being. Thirdly, it establishes a link with
external agencies. At this stage such a link is still fragile and non-
permanent, nevertheless it provides guidance and protection
against destructive aspects. Such destructive aspects are present
within the being, but they are still dormant. We can see the
manifestation of such destructive aspects in "Henry VI" and
"Richard III". Now, however, the being is prepared to deal with
them.

Inception of purification ("Henry VI")

After a short period of access to extraordinary powers, the being of
England experiences a temporary recess. This may be compared to
sea waves at high tide breaking on a shore. The wave reaches
certain points on the shore and then recesses only to come back
moments later with greater strength. The high tide waves break a
path through sand or rocks, so that the next waves may reach
deeper and deeper into the land.

The death of Henry V marked the high tide of the developmental wave. However, England is not capable, as yet, of sustaining the previously experienced state. Therefore, this being has to go through a period of recess before the next crest arrives. It is a period when previously dormant destructive aspects start to mar the being. The presence of these destructive aspects is referred to by Chorus in "Henry V":

> "O England! model to thy inward greatness,
> Like little body with a mighty heart,
> What mightst thou do, that honour would thee do,
> Were all thy children kind and natural!"

The marriage of Henry V and Catherine augmented the inner structure of England. Now England has to go through the purification process that involves the intellect and the heart faculties. The purification is marked by signs of a deeper intuition and an extraordinary power. Traces of intuitive knowledge are the first manifestation of a purified intellect faculty; appearances of extraordinary powers are an indication of a purified heart faculty. These traces and appearances mark the fifth stage of the cycle.

A colour code may be used to indicate the specific objectives of the process. For example, an inner aspect of the intellect faculty is indicated by the colour white, while the colour red is used to mark an inner aspect of the heart faculty. This colour code may help to understand Shakespeare's description of the fifth stage of the cycle, i.e., the inception of the purification of the intellect and the heart faculties.

The disunity between various aspects of England is described as a quarrel between the Duke of York and the Duke of Somerset. The lords select red or white roses to indicate whose claim they believe to be correct. Then, they all watch King Henry VI to see whose side he is going to support. Henry says it shouldn't matter what rose he wears, since he loves both his lords, yet even as he says this, he picks Somerset's red rose. Henry, by aligning himself with Somerset, is setting in motion the Wars of the Roses.

The Wars of the Roses symbolize the purification process. It should be noted that this particular stage of the process requires an active involvement of external (invisible) agencies.

There are two attractions placed in the nature of man. One of these attractions is to lift a man to his higher spheres of functioning. Another attraction is to stoop him down to a kind of low, bestial life. Therefore, two forms of external agencies are needed to bring these attractions into operation. The external agency that brings the attraction to the higher forms of living is often called an angel, and the one which leads man astray is called a demon. In human life, however, there are many combinations of these two extremes that lead to the existence among the agents of many mixes, grades and shades. Therefore, when man enters on a spiritual journey, he encounters a sort of dichotomous situation. On one side, he is provided with new forms of protection, safety, and guidance. On the other side, he is exposed to new distracting challenges. These various attractions are very often described in traditional myths as fairies, spirits, and ghosts.

The presence of the invisible attractions is marked in "Henry VI" by the appearance of Joan of Arc and Talbot. They together represent the disunited roses.

Joan of Arc is a shepherd's daughter. Joan relates that one day, when she was tending her sheep, a vision appeared to her and told her to go to free her country from calamity:

> "God's mother deigned to appear to me
> And in a vision full of majesty
> Will'd me to leave my base vocation
> And free my country from calamity."

This figure showed itself in all its glory; the divine rays brought Joan her beauty. In other words, Joan represents that aspect that has been linked to the invisible agencies. She has been granted a certain insight into the current and future events. For example, she tells the Dauphin of France that she will lead the French troops in breaking the Britons' siege on Orléans. Her words prove to be true. Because of that, the Dauphin of France is very impressed with her.

It should be emphasized that the invisible forces that assist Joan
have been released as a result of the reformation process that has
been symbolically marked by the marriage of Henry V and
Catherine. Joan's very existence is the result of Henry V's
successful victory over France. The appearance of Joan of Arc is an
indication that the purification process has been initiated. She is the
first sign of the process associated with the purification of the
intellect faculty.

Joan has been able to perceive the importance of Henry V.
However, she has not been able to understand the overall process.
Instead, she has convinced herself that it is her time to dominate
the world:

> "Glory is like a circle in the water,
> Which never ceaseth to enlarge itself
> Till by broad spreading it disperse to nought.
> With Henry's death the English circle ends;
> Dispersed are the glories it included.
> Now am I like that proud insulting ship
> Which Caesar and his fortune bare at once."

Joan represents a partially purified but non-reformed aspect of the
intellect faculty. Her appearance is only an indication that the
purification process has been initiated. Her self-centredness leads
her away from the optimal and constructive course of action.
Firstly, she misunderstands her role; secondly, driven by her
egotistic motives, she misuses the capacity that has been given to
her. In other words, this particular aspect that she represents gets
corrupted. For a short period of time she exercises her destructive
influence. Her actions serve to increase the war's viciousness. She
ignores the chivalric code of conduct in her methods of fighting.

Joan's appearance is bound together with the personage of Talbot.
Talbot represents a partially purified but non-reformed aspect of
the heart faculty. The appearance of Talbot is also a result of Henry
V's successful combat of France and his marriage with Catherine.
Talbot, who represents the historical person of John, 7th Lord
Talbot, was a Knight of the Order of the Garter. Talbot is aware of

Joan's origin and her capacity. This is how Talbot describes her:

> "Here, here she comes. I'll have a bout with thee;
> Devil or devil's dam, I'll conjure thee:
> Blood will I draw on thee, thou art a witch,
> And straightway give thy soul to him thou servest."

Talbot fights for the honour of the king and the country. His behaviour and his methods of military leadership are based on the noble conduct of chivalry. He displays extraordinary physical powers. He is so feared by the French that, when he is captured, they have archers guard him even while he sleeps. After being released, he conquers many towns and fortifications in France, until he encounters Joan. Talbot gets trapped on the battlefield at Bordeaux. He is killed in the battle.

After the downfall of Talbot, Joan cannot last any longer either. At a critical moment, she calls for the help of her invisible agents. Previously, Joan described them as the carriers of the glorious rays. At this moment, however, her own corrupted state is such that she sees them as demons. The demons refuse to speak to her. She reminds them that she has always offered her blood to them in exchange for their help. Yet the demons show no interest in her offerings. Joan, without the support of the invisible agents, has to go down. She is captured and burned at the stake.

Talbot and Joan represent another example of two opposite forces that work together towards the same goal. They symbolically illustrate the above-mentioned dichotomous situation. Their function is equivalent to the previously mentioned intellectual duels. However, at this stage, these duels take the form of extraordinary but ineffective experiences. The fate of Joan and Talbot indicate the limited value of such preliminary experiences associated with the awakening of intuitive knowledge and extraordinary powers. Joan has been linked to the invisible forces. However, her still selfish nature does not allow her to use this experience in a constructive way. On the other hand, Talbot's intention is correctly aligned with the overall course of the process. He also has access to extraordinary powers. However, he is lacking perceptive insight into the events. Therefore he is not able to use effectively his chivalric experience. These abilities, as represented by Joan and Talbot, are manifested as mutually destructive because the heart and the intellect are disunited and fogged by dormant negative elements. This being has to get beyond such experiences to continue its progress.

The disappearance of Joan and Talbot allows the self faculty to dominate the being for a brief period of time. This is illustrated by the revolt of the commoners. Cade is the leader of the commoners' revolt. Cade's violence is aimed at those who represent the intellect and the heart faculties. He attacks those who can read or write, and he kills those who support schools. His reign of terror erases any rights of women and makes them fair game for rape. Cade's troops enjoy the pleasures of mob rule more than any promise of progress or freedom. The violence of his army shows the dangers of popular rule: it represents a being that is driven by its self faculty. This revolt represents a situation in which the self faculty is coming back into prominence and takes control over the intellect and the heart faculties.

In "Henry VI", Shakespeare describes the stage in which the purification process has been set in motion. Now it is time to introduce another approach that will allow this being to complete the process.

Completion of purification ("Richard III")

The play "Richard III" describes an approach that aims at diminishing the previously unearthed destructive aspects.

In this approach, the destructive aspects are not confronted directly. Instead, a negative aspect is either implanted or selected from those already present there. This aspect is allowed to manifest itself in its fullest strength. Following spiritual teaching's motto: "like attracts like", all destructive aspects agglomerate around it. Then, all these agglomerated destructive aspects are isolated from others. This leads to a situation where the negative aspects cannot help but turn against their own weaker members. At the same time they are cut off from any access to evolutionary energies. This may be compared to denying them "spiritual oxygen". When they are weakened by this self-induced destruction, they can be diminished more effectively. In a parallel operation, the evolutionary energies are transmitted to constructive aspects. In this way, these constructive aspects get support from the invisible agencies. In other words, seemingly unfortunate events may in reality be part of a certain corrective mechanism. Such a corrective mechanism is quite precisely, step-by-step, described in "Richard III".

After a long civil war between the royal families of York and Lancaster, England enjoys a short period of peace under King Edward IV. But Edward's younger brother, Richard, resents Edward's power and the happiness of those around him. Richard is malicious, power-hungry, and bitter about his physical deformity. Richard is a compelling symbol of intellect faculty in its degenerated form. He can see no other enjoyment but to dominate those who have more pleasing appearances than himself. Richard is a villain. He declares outright in his very first speech that he intends to stop at nothing to achieve his wicked goals. Despite his open allegiance to evil, he is a charismatic and fascinating figure. Because of this, some well-intentioned characters of the play cannot help but sympathize with him, or even be attracted to him. For example, Lady Anne, who has an explicit knowledge of his wickedness, allows herself to be seduced by his brilliant wordplay, his skilful argumentation, his relentless pursuit of his selfish desires. She agrees to marry him.

Richard begins to aspire secretly to the crown and torments himself with ideas about how to get it:

> "Why, I can smile, and murder whiles I smile,
> And cry 'Content' to that which grieves my heart,
> And wet my cheeks with artificial tears,
> And frame my face to all occasions.
> I'll drown more sailors than the mermaid shall;
> I'll slay more gazers than the basilisk;
> I'll play the orator as well as Nestor,
> Deceive more slily than Ulysses could,
> And, like a Sinon, take another Troy.
> I can add colours to the chameleon,

Change shapes with Proteus for advantages,
And set the murderous Machiavel to school.
Can I do this, and cannot get a crown?
Tut, were it farther off, I'll pluck it down."

There are many people who stand between him and the crown. Richard decides to kill anyone who stands in his way and manages to become the king of England. However his reign of terror causes the common people of England to fear and loathe him, and gradually he alienates nearly all the noblemen of the court. When rumours begin to spread around about a challenger to the throne who is gathering forces in France, most of the noblemen defect to join his forces. The challenger is the Earl of Richmond, a descendant of a secondary branch of the Lancaster family. In the meantime, Richard tries to consolidate his power. He has his wife Anne murdered so that he can marry his niece. Such an alliance would further enhance his grasp of the throne. At this point, however, Richard starts to lose control of the events.

Richmond invades England. The night before the decisive battle, as both leaders sleep, they begin to dream. This scene illustrates an example of a situation in which the invisible agencies get involved in the process. A parade of ghosts of everyone whom Richard has murdered comes across the stage. First, each ghost stops to speak to Richard. Each condemns him bitterly for his or her death, tells him that he will be killed in battle the next morning, and orders him to despair and die. Then each ghost moves away and speaks to the sleeping Richmond, telling him that they are on his side and that Richmond will rule England and father a race of kings. In a similar manner, eleven ghosts move across the stage. Richard wakes out of his sleep sweating and gasping. For the first time Richard is truly terrified.

Afterwards, Richard speaks brusquely to his remaining supporters. At that moment he is essentially isolated from his courtiers and his family members. As a result of his malicious nature, he has killed anyone who became close to him; his brothers, nephews, and even his own wife are all dead at his hand; his mother has cursed and abandoned him; and even Buckingham, who was once his closest friend, has been sent to execution. Richard has gradually destroyed all his close relationships. Now he is still in power, but he is alone.

In his battle speech Richard mocks the enemy soldiers, calling them "a scum of Bretons and base lackey peasants". His troops outnumber Richmond's by three to one. Therefore, Richard is sure that might makes right, and that:

> "Conscience is but a word that cowards use,
> Devised at first to keep the strong in awe:
> Our strong arms be our conscience, swords our law."

In contrast, Richmond, very much Richard's opposite, claims to fight for honour. He is gracious and friendly to both his noblemen and his soldiers. Richmond asks his men to remember the beauty of the land that they are saving from a tyrant, and the wives and children whom they will be making free. He reminds his men that he himself will die in battle if he cannot win, and if he does succeed then all his soldiers will be rewarded. Richmond brings back the chivalry, the code of proper conduct. In other words, chivalry rises again. This is possible now, because Richmond has been able to combine together the chivalric experience and the support of the invisible agencies.

Richard is killed in the battle. Richmond is crowned King Henry VII. Promising a new era of peace for England, the new king is betrothed to young Elizabeth in order to unite the warring houses of Lancaster and York. The red and the white roses are united. This time, however, the reformed and purified being is capable of sustaining the unity of the faculties.

Activation of permanent consciousness ("Henry VIII")

The play "Henry VIII" describes the completion of the cycle. When the negative aspects have been diminished, then the being is capable of uniting all remaining constructive aspects. Such a unification and harmonization lead to the final stage of the cycle, when the being can experience its fullest potential. At this stage, all major aspects of the being are becoming conscious of the overall purpose.

The play "Henry VIII" describes a significant moment in English history, namely England's religious break from Rome and the Catholic Church. In 1531, King Henry VIII, disappointed that his wife Katherine had borne him no male heirs, decided to divorce her. His advisors argued that the marriage was invalid, but the Pope ruled against the divorce. Nevertheless, Henry divorced his wife and married Anne Boleyn.

It is obvious that the character of Henry VIII is fully aware of the rule "right people, right place, and right time". Henry does not interfere with the flow of events. He only acts when a forceful occasion requires his intervention. For example, he does not intervene when Buckingham, his wife Katherine, or his right-hand man Wolsey are in trouble. However, he gets actively involved when the courtiers plot against Cranmer. It is the first time that we see him as an active king. Never before has Henry seemed to pay attention to the plots churning behind the scenes that place people in and out of his favour. However, Henry is galvanized to save Cranmer. Why does Henry protect Cranmer? The answer to this question provides the key to the understanding of the entire series of Shakespeare's History Plays. Namely, Cranmer has to play a critical role in the final stage of the process. All characters that have been previously eliminated had to go because their presence was blocking the circumstances leading to the ultimate outcome of the process: the birth of Elizabeth. Buckingham had to go because he believed that he had a claim to the throne; Katherine had to go because she did not give birth to the right heirs; and Wolsey had to go because he opposed Henry's marriage to Anne. Cranmer, on the other hand, has to be present at the birth and baptize the newborn child. It may be presumed that Cranmer represents the aspect that provides a link to the evolutionary transmission chain. This particular link was engrafted onto England some 400 years before. It is the same link that was provided by the Bastard in "King John". In this way the link may be transferred to Elizabeth. This is clearly indicated in the last scene when Cranmer baptizes Elizabeth and announces her future greatness:

"Let me speak, sir,

For heaven now bids me; and the words I utter
Let none think flattery, for they'll find 'em truth.
This royal infant - heaven still move about her! -
Though in her cradle, yet now promises
Upon this land a thousand thousand blessings,
Which time shall bring to ripeness

...

She shall be loved and fear'd: her own shall bless her;
Her foes shake like a field of beaten corn,
And hang their heads with sorrow: good grows with her:
In her days every man shall eat in safety,
Under his own vine, what he plants; and sing
The merry songs of peace to all his neighbours:
God shall be truly known; and those about her
From her shall read the perfect ways of honour ... "

Cranmer says that the infant holds great promise for England, and few now can imagine the great things she will accomplish. She will know truth, she will be loved and feared, and she will be a great ruler. When she dies, she will be reborn like a phoenix in her heir, and all her good attributes will carry on in the next ruler. He predicts that all Elizabeth's good traits will be carried on in her heir, James I, the next king of England. In other words, Cranmer announces the actualization of the "unconquerable force of England" and the "inner greatness" that was predicted by the Bastard in "King John" and by Chorus in "Henry V".

Henry reaffirms his overall goal by saying that with this child he finally feels he has accomplished something great. He looks forward to seeing what she will do from his future post in heaven.

As has been mentioned earlier, at this final stage of development all major aspects of the being are becoming conscious of the overall purpose. Regardless of their own individual fate, they all accept graciously the chain of events, even if this means their own fall or death. For example, when Katherine hears of Wolsey's death, she is able to forgive his bad treatment of her. Then Katherine stresses her own humility to the king. Humility and forgiveness come to all those cast off by the king.

It helps to understand these events if the readers realize that "Elizabeth" represents the ultimate outcome of the History Plays. She symbolizes the goal of this particular cycle. The being of England achieves its objective at the moment of Elizabeth's birth. She is the hidden treasure that is to be found. Elizabeth is a symbol of the reformed and purified intellect faculty. Elizabeth's birth is the goal of the process described in the History Plays.

The being of England achieves its perfected state. Now this being can enter onto the next cycle of the evolutionary spiral. This applies both to the individual being that is called "England", as well as to a certain fraction of European society.

Beginning of a modern cycle

It was during Elizabeth's reign that some of Shakespeare's plays were first released. This is an important factor that should be taken into consideration when reading the History Plays. The titles of these plays encompass the reigns of seven kings: King John, Richard II, Henry IV, Henry V, Henry VI, Richard III and Henry VIII. It may be assumed that the release of Shakespeare's History Plays during the reigns of Elizabeth I and James I was an announcement to the world that a certain evolutionary cycle of Western European society had been completed. This evolutionary cycle came to fruition in England, among other regions, through the more developed attitudes of the rulers of the time.

Elizabeth I was Queen of England from 1559 until her death in 1603. Elizabeth was the sixth and final monarch of the Tudor dynasty. During the Tudor dynasty, England was transformed from a comparatively weak ignoble backwater of Europe still immersed in the Middle Ages, into a powerful Renaissance state. In the coming centuries, England would dominate much of the world and English colonization of North America would take place. Elizabeth's reign is referred to as the Elizabethan era or the Golden Age.

The evolutionary stages that are described in the History Plays prepared the ground for the next, more advanced cycles.

Historically, one may look at it as a certain spiritual quantum leap in Western Europe.

Conclusion

The History Plays describe a specific sequence and main features of the evolutionary process that has been induced by an injection of evolutionary energy. Once the process had been initiated, it continued to its completion.

In his other plays, Shakespeare illustrates more complex evolutionary sequences. In accordance with the natural capacities and character of a disciple, a guide may optimize the sequence of required experiences. Therefore, certain stages will be induced in some disciples, while others may require a different sequence, or even may be prevented from certain experiences. These various stages may overlap; they may phase out, and later on they may phase in again. Two or more stages may appear at the same time. The time period required for the completion of each of the stages is not fixed either, it may vary from one stage to the next. The guide may compress the time, if required, and he may load a few stages into an event lasting a few days. Shakespeare pointed this out by presenting "Henry IV" in two parts, and "Henry VI" in three parts.

The History Plays are based on a template that is used in all other Shakespeare's plays. Each of Shakespeare's plays is related to one or several stages illustrated in the History Plays. In other words, the remaining 27 Shakespeare plays are parts of the whole. They all describe various states and stages of the evolutionary process.

As mentioned in the introduction, in the early 60s, the play "Henry V" was used to outline the program of a new phase of spiritual teaching in the West. It may be presumed that this new western phase corresponded symbolically to the stage of Henry V, but on a higher notch of the evolutionary spiral. It is probable that the initiates, as individuals, as a group, and as citizens of the West, were to experience the states corresponding to those described in "Henry V".

If the evolutionary cycle described in the History Plays was focused on Western Europe, then it is quite possible that some aspects of the activity initiated in the early 60s were projected on a much larger scale. This may be deduced from the events that followed: the fall of the Berlin Wall, the disintegration of the Soviet block, the collapse of the Soviet Union and the creation of the European Union.

If the evolutionary sequence described in Shakespeare's plays is applicable to today's stage of the evolutionary cycle, then one could expect that the stage of "Henry V" would be followed or overlapped with the stages described in "Henry VI", "Richard III", and "Henry VIII". Such an evolutionary sequence would indicate that right now, the initiates, as well as humanity in general, face new and formidable challenges on their path towards further development.

It is quite possible that an outline of the current spiritual teaching program would also be announced by releasing a play, a book, or a movie.

CHAPTER 2

Roman Evolutionary Cycle

Wes Jamroz

50

2.1 Initial Stage in "Coriolanus"

Introduction

The play "Coriolanus" is based on the life of the legendary Roman general Caius Martius Coriolanus. The play follows the story of Coriolanus as described by Plutarch in "Lives of the Noble Greeks and Romans".

"Coriolanus" may not appear to be a great play. It may seem lacking in depth. Its characters are not multi-dimensional. Its title character, Caius Martius, rarely pauses to reflect or reveal the motives behind his actions. In this way, he is shallower than other Shakespearean heroes. For these reasons "Coriolanus" has not been considered one of Shakespeare's most popular plays.

However, there are a couple of factors that should be considered when analyzing the play which might help to explain this apparent deficiency. The first factor is related to the historical background of the play. The historical Caius Martius Coriolanus lived in the 5th century BC. The action of "Coriolanus" is set in the aftermath of the fall of Tarquin, the last tyrannical king of Rome who ruled between 535 and 510 BC. Therefore, the action of the play takes place earlier than the events described in the other plays of the Roman tetralogy, i.e., "Julius Caesar", "Antony and Cleopatra" and "Titus Andronicus".

The second factor is related to the timing of the release of "Coriolanus". "Coriolanus" is one of Shakespeare's later plays; it is estimated that it was written in 1608. Therefore "Coriolanus" was released at a time when Shakespeare's most sophisticated characters already were created and fully developed. This fact in itself provides an additional pointer that may help to understand the overall function of "Coriolanus".

As indicated previously, each of Shakespeare's plays is part of a whole. All of the plays are interlinked. Together they form a narrative that describes the most recent episodes of human evolution. It is a story that illustrates how European civilization was directed and implemented. It is in this context that the role of "Coriolanus" can be understood. Namely, "Coriolanus" is written as a reference play. The play defines the starting point for the Roman tetralogy. Therefore, the play's simplicity, the plainness of its language, and the shallowness of its characters are deliberate. "Coriolanus" may be fully appreciated only if it is analyzed in the context of the other Roman plays.

Technical background

There is an evolutionary plan for the planet Earth, and its history, apparently haphazard and random, is not the blind, accidental process it seems. The evolution of organic life was directed, and in the same way, the human race continues to be guided, encouraged or restrained into alignment with the universal design.

Evolutionary progress was achieved by making available on the planetary scene a succession of energies, each higher in its developmental potentiality than the one before. Constructive, vital, automatic, conscious, creative, unitive, and supracognitive energies were switched in turn[2]. Constructive, vital, and automatic energies had given rise to mineral, vegetable, and animal forms of life, respectively. Consequently, the release of conscious and creative energies led to the appearance of modern man. These various modes of energies may be compared to different kinds of "food" that, at different times and at different places on the planet, were made available to mankind. These energies are like commodities; their amount is limited and they may become scarce if they are not used correctly. Symbolically, the situations of temporary developmental deficiencies are described as "famines".

Switching-in conscious energy allowed for the proper alignment (reformation) of man's manifest faculties, while creative energy led to the activation of inner layers of the faculties (purification).

---

[2] Symbolically, the release of each mode of evolutionary energy corresponds to a new spiritual millennium. This is why the phrase "seven thousand years" is used to refer to the mythical age of the world.

Unitive energy, which is the second highest evolutionary energy in the galaxy, allows for the unification of the inner layers of the manifest faculties.

The unified inner layers can be transmuted into a new organ of supracognitive perception. Supracognitive energy acts as a catalyst for the activation of this inner organ of perception. The organ of inner perception allows man to perceive and act in accordance with the design at the level of the Realm, i.e., beyond ordinary space-time limitations. The organ of supracognitive perception existed already in eternity and was required to be actualized in time. Though latent since man emerged from his primate ancestry, it is an organ of experience that has only intermittently been active in certain exceptional individuals. Man is due to inherit it one day as part of his total experience.

Modern man has been faced with a very difficult challenge to accommodate these new potentialities that were offered to him. The sequence and the effects of these switching-ins suggest that each new mode of energies is made available while man is still struggling to come to terms with the previous ones. Therefore, the developmental techniques and approaches have to be adjusted in such a way as to be compatible with these various energies as well as with the specific characteristics of the localities and people that are directly exposed to these evolutionary impacts. The custodians of the process have kept adapting their teaching techniques in order to meet these challenges.

Shakespeare's plays describe the evolutionary adjustments that were implemented during the period between the 10th century BC and the 16th century AD. These adjustments were implemented through several evolutionary branches that were activated in various parts of Western Europe.

"Coriolanus" describes an earlier stage of the evolutionary process. At the time of "Coriolanus", man had not yet experienced the effects of properly functioning manifest faculties. It is in this sense that "Coriolanus" provides a reference point for the more advanced evolutionary stages that are described in the other Roman plays. This is the reason why "Coriolanus" is written in such a way as to present Rome as a relatively simplistic and unsophisticated being. The characters that appear in "Coriolanus" have not been exposed to higher evolutionary energies yet; therefore they are purposely presented as inwardly one-dimensional and unrefined.

Storyline

The play starts in Rome, shortly after the expulsion of the last Tarquin king. There are riots on the streets after stores of grain were withheld from ordinary citizens. The rioters are particularly angry with Caius Martius, a Roman general, whom they blame for the grain being taken away. The rioters encounter a patrician named Menenius as well as Caius Martius himself. Menenius tries to calm the rioters, while Caius Martius is openly contemptuous, and says that the plebeians are not worthy of the grain because they do not responsibly serve their city. Two of the tribunes of Rome, Brutus and Sicinius, privately denounce Caius Martius. At this moment, news arrives that a Volscian army is in the field and is ready to lead an assault on the city. Caius Martius leaves Rome to fight against the Volscian invaders.

The Roman army is commanded by Cominius with Caius Martius as his deputy. While Cominius takes his soldiers to meet the Volscian army, Caius Martius leads a sortie against the Volscian city of Corioli. The siege of Corioli is initially unsuccessful, but Caius Martius is able to force open the gates of the city, and the Romans conquer it. Even though he is exhausted from the fighting, Caius Martius marches quickly to join Cominius and fights the other Volscian force. The commander of the Volscian army, Tullus Aufidius, has fought against Caius Martius on several occasions, and considers him a bloody enemy. Caius Martius and Aufidius meet in single combat, which only ends when Aufidius' own soldiers drag him away from the battle.

In recognition of his bravery, Cominius gives Caius Martius the honorific surname of Coriolanus. When they return to Rome, Caius Martius' mother, Volumnia, encourages her son to run for the position of Consul of Rome. Caius Martius is hesitant to do this, but he bows to his mother's wishes. He easily wins the support of the Roman Senate, and seems at first to have won over the commoners as well. However, Brutus and Sicinius scheme to undo Caius Martius, and they stir up another riot against him. Faced with opposition, Caius Martius flies into a rage, and rails against the concept of popular rule. He compares the notion of allowing plebeians to have power over the patricians to allowing "crows to peck the eagles". The two tribunes condemn Caius Martius as a traitor. Caius Martius is banished from Rome.

After being exiled from Rome, Caius Martius seeks out Aufidius in the Volscian capital of Antium and tells him that he will lead the Volscian army to victory against Rome. Aufidius and the Volscian's Senate embrace Caius Martius and allow him to lead a new assault on the city.

Rome, panicking, tries desperately to persuade Caius Martius to halt his crusade for vengeance, but both Cominius and Menenius fail. Finally, Volumnia is sent to meet with her son, along with Caius Martius' wife -Virgilia, his young son, and Valeria, a Roman noblewoman. Volumnia succeeds in dissuading her son from destroying Rome, and Caius Martius instead concludes a peace treaty between the Volscians and the Romans.

When Caius Martius returns to the Volscian capital, conspirators organized by Aufidius, kill him for his betrayal.

Rome: 5th century BC

In the History Plays it is indicated that the universe is arranged according to a design that is based upon the principle of hierarchy. This hierarchy is compared to the patterns observed in nature, among plants, animals, and heavenly bodies. It has also been indicated that a spiritually developed man is superior to other men. It is in this context that the notion of a "king" or "monarchy" is used in Shakespeare's plays. In other words, the concept of kingdom is used to illustrate the inner structure of properly functioning manifest faculties. On the other hand, the popular-rule type of governance is used to present a rather intermittent and malfunctioning being, which is driven by a corrupted self faculty.

However, it would be naïve and erroneous to draw from such a symbolic presentation any conclusions related to political or social preferences.

"Coriolanus" describes Rome in the 5th century BC. At that time Rome was in transition from a previous tyrannical monarchy into a republic, which was to be an intermediary stage toward the future Empire. Shakespeare selected this particular historical time to describe the period when man was capable of no more than minimal consciousness, yet was confronted with creativity. This corresponds to the time when Rome had not developed a properly functioning intellect faculty, yet it faced unknown and unfamiliar experiences of extraordinary powers associated with inner aspects of the heart faculty.

Element of creative energy
Virgilia represents an element of creative energy. She is Caius Martius' wife. Virgilia is the most gentle of all characters. Shakespeare uses Valeria, a rather harsh woman, to emphasize Virgilia's softness and kindness. On several occasions Virgilia distinguishes herself by being ... eloquently silent. In this way Shakespeare indicates that at the time of Coriolanus this element was still partially dormant. This element was made available to Rome, but was not fully assimilated yet. First, the being of Rome would have to develop the properly aligned manifest faculties.

Underdeveloped intellect faculty
The first requirement for the proper functioning of the being is to align the manifest faculties in such a way that the intellect controls the heart and the self. The main difficulty of Rome is that it lacks a properly developed intellect faculty. Namely, the role of the intellect faculty has been diluted by delegating its functions to a substitute in the form of the Senate and the tribunes.

At this stage of the evolutionary development, traces of consciousness are indicated by the being's awareness of the need for the correct governance of its manifest faculties. As discussed in the History Plays, this stage corresponds to the "preliminary realization".

Menenius, a Roman patrician, represents this aspect of the intellect faculty that carries some minimal consciousness induced by the previously released conscious energy. He is aware of the need for correct governance. Menenius is a gifted spokesman and has the reputation of having great wit. However, he is rather weak and his role is limited to defending Caius Martius against the tribunes.

Menenius tries to convey to the plebeians the importance of correct governance by telling them a parable about the arrangement of various organs within the human body. He compares the correct functioning of the manifest faculties to the digestive system. In Menenius' parable, the stomach itself describes its function in the following way:

> "... I receive the general food at first,
> Which you do live upon; and fit it is,
> Because I am the store-house and the shop
> Of the whole body: but, if you do remember,
> I send it through the rivers of your blood,
> Even to the court, the heart, to the seat o' the brain;
> And, through the cranks and offices of man,
> The strongest nerves and small inferior veins
> From me receive that natural competency
> Whereby they live.
>   ...
> 'Though all at once cannot
> See what I do deliver out to each,
> Yet I can make my audit up, that all
> From me do back receive the flour of all,
> And leave me but the bran."

Menenius explains to the plebeians that the Senate, similarly to the stomach, serves as the storehouse and the collecting-place for the nutrients and then dispenses them throughout the rest of the body:

> "The senators of Rome are this good belly,
> And you the mutinous members."

And then he spells out what the role of the plebeians is:

"You, the great toe of this assembly."

The stomach's parable is used here to illustrate the current evolutionary state of Rome. As mentioned above, Rome is capable of no more than minimal consciousness, yet it is confronted with creativity. In order to take the full benefit of this new kind of food, a properly functioning digestive system needs to be developed.

It may help to grasp Shakespeare's concept of "different kinds of food" offered to mankind at different times to recall the description of a corresponding effect associated with unitive energy. While the effect of exposure to conscious energy is compared in "Coriolanus" to the digestion of corn, the exposure to unitive energy is paralleled by Sir John Falstaff's in "Henry IV" to the drinking of wine. The "drinking of wine" is used as a technical term to describe the effect of the exposure to unitive energy of love. It is in this sense that "wine" is needed to purify and unify the inner faculties. Shakespeare discreetly indicates that Rome at the time of Coriolanus is still spiritually "asleep" and is not ready yet for "wine":

> "Wine, wine, wine! What service
> is here! I think our fellows are asleep."

First, therefore, the manifest faculties have to be correctly aligned. And this is Rome's current challenge. Menenius tries to explain to the plebeians, and to the audience, that as long as Rome is incapable of properly distributing the "corn" it will suffer from developmental indigestion that will disturb its correct growth. In this particular case, the indigestion has already led to an atrophied growth of its heart faculty.

Atrophied heart faculty

The heart faculty is the strongest faculty of the being of Rome. However, this faculty is inadequately outgrown. Caius Martius, his mother Volumnia, his young son Martius, and a Roman noblewoman Valeria represent it. The fact that Virgilia is Caius Martius's wife indicates that creative energy has been attached to the Roman heart.

Caius Martius is a brave general, fearsome in battle, and extremely honourable. He is also overly proud, inflexible, and stubborn. These features, combined with a fierce contempt for the tribunes and the plebeians make him an incongruent aspect of Rome. Despite his unquestionable skills and abilities there is no place for him among the Romans. There is no adequate environment or mechanism that would allow harnessing properly the skills that have been endowed in this particular aspect of Rome. One may suppose that these extraordinary skills have been prematurely activated and led to its deformed outgrowth. Menenius compares him to a cumbersome dragon with wings that atrophically evolved from a "creeping thing":

> "There is difference between a grub and a butterfly;
> yet your butterfly was a grub. This Marcius is grown
> from man to dragon: he has wings; he's more than a
> creeping thing."

Caius Martius, despite his extraordinary military skills, acts impulsively and erratically. Shakespeare clearly underlines Caius Martius' imbalanced behaviour in an episode of the battle of Corioli. When offered awards after he single-handedly defeated the Volscians at Corioli, Caius Martius refused to accept anything. But then he made the following request to Cominius:

> "I sometime lay here in Corioli
> At a poor man's house; he used me kindly:
> He cried to me; I saw him prisoner;
> But then Aufidius was with in my view,
> And wrath o'erwhelm'd my pity: I request you
> To give my poor host freedom."

And when Cominius granted him his wish, Caius Martius could not even remember the name of the man whose life he wanted to save:

> "By Jupiter! forgot.
> I am weary; yea, my memory is tired.
> Have we no wine here?"

Volumnia, Caius Martius' mother, represents another aspect of the heart faculty. Because of the lack of a leading intellect faculty within the being of Rome, Volumnia tries to fill this vacuum. Her ambition is to govern Rome through her son. She raises her son to be a great soldier, and then she desires to make him the Consul of Rome. In this indirect way she hopes to exercise her influence and power. Volumnia's ambitious actions transgress the requirements for the proper functioning of the being.

There is another obstacle that prevents Rome to operate efficiently. It is its corrupted self faculty.

Tribunes and plebeians
A corrupted self faculty refers to an arrangement where this faculty exerts control over the heart and the intellect. The plebeians and their tribunes represent the corrupted self faculty.

In the aftermath of the famine, the plebeians demand the right to set their own price for the city's grain supply. Here is a sample of the citizens' attitude toward Caius Martius, who openly opposes their demands:

> "Let us kill him, and we'll have corn at our own price.
> Is't a verdict?"

The ruling aristocracy, or patricians, in response to these protests grants the plebeians five positions in the tribunes. These five tribunes further dilute the already weakened intellect faculty. This augmentation of the governing body provokes the fury of Caius Martius who compares this situation to "bringing in the crows to peck the eagles". Caius Martius angrily addresses the tribunes:

> "… He that trusts to you,
> Where he should find you lions, finds you hares;
> Where foxes, geese: you are no surer, no,
> Than is the coal of fire upon the ice,
> Or hailstone in the sun. Your virtue is
> To make him worthy whose offence subdues him
> And curse that justice did it.
> Who deserves greatness
> Deserves your hate; and your affections are

A sick man's appetite, who desires most that
Which would increase his evil. He that depends
Upon your favours swims with fins of lead
And hews down oaks with rushes. Hang ye! Trust Ye?
With every minute you do change a mind,
And call him noble that was now your hate,
Him vile that was your garland."

Two tribunes, Brutus and Sicinius, are supposed to serve in the government as the representatives of the plebeians. However, their actions are driven by their self-importance and self-interest. They are power hungry and exploiting, or as Menenius comments, they act as:

"... the herdsmen of the beastly plebeians."

The plebeians are irresponsible and driven by their upstart passions. They are fickle and cowardly. Here it is how a plebeian himself describes the common people's unfocussed and confused behaviour:

"We have been called so of many; not that our heads
are some brown, some black, some auburn, some bald,
but that our wits are so diversely coloured: and
truly I think if all our wits were to issue out of
one skull, they would fly east, west, north, south,
and their consent of one direct way should be at
once to all the points o' the compass."

The current situation of Rome is further explained in the above-referred stomach's parable. In this parable, the other member of the body rebelled against the stomach:

"There was a time when all the body's members
Rebell'd against the belly, thus accused it:
That only like a gulf it did remain
I' the midst o' the body, idle and unactive,
Still cupboarding the viand, never bearing
Like labour with the rest, where the other instruments
Did see and hear, devise, instruct, walk, feel,

> And, mutually participate, did minister
> Unto the appetite and affection common
> Of the whole body."

The being cannot function efficiently with such a type of governing arrangement. With such an inner structure, Rome may be described as an upside down city:

> "That is the way to lay the city flat;
> To bring the roof to the foundation,
> And bury all, which yet distinctly ranges,
> In heaps and piles of ruin."

Therefore, a corrective action is required to straighten up the situation.

Corrective action

A corrective action may be realized through the uplifting of an aspect that is capable of taking on the leading role. Firstly, however, such a selected aspect would have to be prepared for such a role by going through a series of trials. In Shakespeare's plays, the inception of such preparatory trials is usually marked by banishment. If a being is linked to the evolutionary transmission chain, then such a banished character ends up wandering through a heath or a forest. It is there that he, or she, goes through uplifting experiences. If there is no such forest, then the corrective action is limited to the eradication of the most distractive aspects. Such eradication may protect a being against its spiritual extinction. The elimination of the most incongruent aspects may be realized through a secondary layer of the being.

The secondary layer of Rome is represented by the Volscian city of Antium. Outwardly both cities appear to be hostile to each other. In reality they are both integral parts of the same being. The city of Antium, with its Senate and fickle plebeians, is like a mirror reflection of Rome. A link between Rome and Antium is formed through a relationship between Caius Martius and Aufidius. The link between the two layers is based on a mix of admiration, envy, and hate. Aufidius is a general of the Volscians and he is the leading aspect of the secondary layer. Caius Martius admires Aufidius as a worthy adversary:

> "They have a leader,
> Tullus Aufidius, that will put you to 't.
> I sin in envying his nobility,
> And were I any thing but what I am,
> I would wish me only he."

Similar feelings toward Caius Martius are expressed by Aufidius:

> "O Marcius, Marcius!
> Each word thou hast spoke hath weeded from my heart
> A root of ancient envy. If Jupiter
> Should from yond cloud speak divine things,
> And say 'Tis true, I'ld not believe them more
> Than thee, all noble Marcius. Let me twine
> Mine arms about that body, where against
> My grained ash an hundred times hath broke
> And scarr'd the moon with splinters: here I clip
> The anvil of my sword, and do contest
> As hotly and as nobly with thy love
> As ever in ambitious strength I did
> Contend against thy valour."

The readers may note that there is no active evolutionary impulse within Rome. This is further marked by the famine and shortages of "grain". In other words, the previously released impulse of conscious energy has already been expended and the element of creative energy is still partially dormant. All of these indicate that Rome is still disconnected from the evolutionary transmission chain. In such a situation the corrective action is limited to the eradication of the most incongruent aspect. The banishment of Caius Martius marks the moment of instigation of the corrective action. As there is no "forest", therefore Caius Martius goes to the city of Antium. While in Antium, Caius Martius is eliminated. In this way Rome is prevented, at least temporarily, from further deterioration.

Conclusion

"Coriolanus" describes the evolutionary stage of 5th century BC Rome. Rome was to serve as a seed of the future European civilization. Let's take a closer look at the state of this predecessor of the modern Europe.

The most conscious aspect of the intellect faculty is represented by Menenius. Menenius, as indicated above, is quite weak and politically impotent. The fact that Volumnia has been able to exercise a greater influence than Menenius - further underlines his limitations. One may expect that the influence of the self faculty will be further strengthened and will lead to the gradual corruption of the being.

There is also an indication that an ingredient of cruelty is cultivated within this being. Caius Martius' young son represents such an ingredient. Valeria's fascination with Young Martius, who caught a butterfly and tore it to pieces with his teeth, is a sign of such a tendency:

> "I saw him run after a gilded
> butterfly: and when he caught it, he let it go
> again; and after it again; and over and over he
> comes, and again; catched it again; or whether his
> fall enraged him, or how 'twas, he did so set his
> teeth and tear it; O, I warrant it, how he mammocked it!"

This seed of cruelty will have detrimental effect on the entire Roman cycle.

In summary, 5th century BC Rome has not yet developed a properly functioning intellect faculty. At the same time, Rome's overall functionality is distracted by the presence of dominant aspects of the self faculty. As the previously released evolutionary impulse has been expended, there is no adequate environment that would allow harnessing the powers endowed within the heart faculty. In other words, there is no indication that the Rome of "Coriolanus" would be able to make any evolutionary progress. Yet, in the 1st century BC, Rome became the centre of an empire stretching from Britain to North Africa and from Spain to Persia. This would indicate that something significant took place in Rome between the 5th and the 1st centuries BC. This "something" greatly enhanced the evolutionary state of Rome.

It may be presumed that sometime between the 5th century and the 1st century BC Rome was exposed to a significant evolutionary event. Shakespeare would not allude to such a possibility without explaining it in a greater detail. Namely, the details related to this evolutionary event are described in "Julius Caesar".

2.2 Release of Unitive Energy in "Julius Caesar"

Introduction

"Julius Caesar" portrays the conspiracy against the Roman dictator Julius Caesar, his assassination and its aftermath. It is the second play of Shakespeare's Roman tetralogy. Similarly to "Coriolanus", the direct source for the play was Plutarch's "Lives of the Noble Greeks and Romans".

Julius Caesar lived in 100 - 44 BC. He was a Roman military and political leader and one of the most influential men in history. He played a critical role in the transformation of the Roman Republic into the Roman Empire.

The Roman Empire succeeded the 500-year-old Roman Republic (510 BC - 1st century BC), which had been weakened by the civil war of Julius Caesar against Pompey the Great. Several dates are commonly proposed to mark the transition from Republic to Empire, including the date of Julius Caesar's appointment as perpetual dictator (44 BC), the victory of Caesar's heir Octavius at the Battle of Actium (31 BC), and the Roman Senate's granting Octavius the honorific title of *Augustus* (27 BC).

Rome's influence upon the law, technology, language, government, military, and architecture of the civilizations that arose from this ancient ancestor continues to this day.

Technical background

As indicated in the analysis of "Coriolanus", sometime between the 5th century and the 1st century BC, Rome was exposed to an evolutionary event. Shakespeare identifies this event with the release of unitive energy.

The play "Julius Caesar" describes the effect of the first encounter of mankind with unitive energy. It was a very significant moment in man's recent evolutionary experience. Shakespeare indicates that this happened before man was ready for it. As has been pointed out in "Coriolanus", at that time man was only marginally conscious and only a minute spark of creativity had crystallized in him. Yet, he was now being faced with the challenge of accommodating the second highest energy in the galaxy.

Storyline

Julius Caesar has just defeated his archrival - the Roman general Pompey. During the triumphal parade a soothsayer calls out to Caesar "beware the Ides of March", but Caesar ignores him and proceeds with his victory celebration.

Marcus Brutus is Caesar's close friend. His ancestors were famed for driving the tyrannical king Tarquin from Rome. Brutus allows himself to be cajoled into joining a group of conspiring senators because of a growing suspicion, implanted by Cassius, that Caesar intends to turn republican Rome into a monarchy under his own rule. Brutus finds letters in his house apparently written by Roman citizens worried that Caesar has become too powerful. The letters have in fact been forged and planted by Cassius, who knows that if Brutus believes that it is the people's will, he will support a plot to remove Caesar from power. Cassius arrives at Brutus' home with a group of conspirators. The men agree to lure Caesar from his house and kill him.

That night Rome is plagued with violent weather and a variety of bad omens and portents.

On the following morning, which is the Ides of March, Caesar prepares to go to the Senate. His wife, Calphurnia, begs him not to go, describing her recent nightmare. Caesar refuses to yield to fear and insists on going about his daily business. Finally, Calphurnia convinces him to stay home - if not out of caution, then as a favour to her. But Decius, one of the conspirators, arrives and convinces Caesar that Calphurnia has misinterpreted her dream. Caesar departs to the Senate in the company of the conspirators.

As Caesar proceeds through the streets toward the Senate, the citizen Artemidorus hands him a letter warning him about the conspirators. Caesar refuses to read the letter, saying that his personal safety is his last priority. At the Senate, the conspirators speak to Caesar, bowing at his feet and encircling him. One by one, they stab him to death.

Antony, Caesar's friend, weeps over Caesar's body. He shakes hands with the conspirators appearing to make a gesture of conciliation. When Antony asks why they killed Caesar, Brutus replies that he will explain their purpose in a funeral oration. Antony asks to be allowed to speak over the body as well. Brutus grants his permission, though Cassius remains suspicious of Antony.

Brutus and Cassius go to the Forum to speak to the public. Brutus declares to the masses that though he loved Caesar, he loves Rome more, and Caesar's ambition posed a danger to Roman liberty. The speech placates the crowd. Then Antony appears with Caesar's body, and Brutus departs after turning the pulpit over to him. Repeatedly referring to Brutus as an honourable man, Antony's speech becomes increasingly sarcastic. Antony points out that Caesar brought much wealth and glory to Rome, and three times turned down offers of the crown. Antony then produces Caesar's will that bequeaths a sum of money to every citizen and orders that his private garden be made public. The crowd becomes enraged that this generous man lies dead. Calling Brutus and Cassius traitors, the masses set off to drive them from the city.

Octavius, Caesar's adopted son and appointed successor, arrives in Rome and forms a three-person coalition with Antony and Lepidus. They prepare to fight Cassius and Brutus, who are raising armies outside the city. That night, when Cassius and Brutus prepare for battle with Antony and Octavius, the ghost of Caesar appears to Brutus, announcing that Brutus will meet him again on the battlefield.

During the battle Cassius witnesses his own men fleeing and hears that Brutus' men are not performing effectively. Cassius despairs and orders one of his men to kill him with his own sword. He dies proclaiming that Caesar is avenged.

Brutus learns of the death of Cassius with a heavy heart. When his army loses, doom appears imminent. Brutus asks one of his men to hold his sword while he impales himself on it. He dies saying that Caesar can rest satisfied.

Octavius and Antony arrive. Antony speaks over Brutus' body, calling him the noblest Roman of all. Octavius orders that Brutus be buried in the most honourable way.

Rome: 1st century BC

Shakespeare uses the historical figure of Julius Caesar to symbolically illustrate a spiritual guide who is charged with the incredibly difficult task of facilitating the utilization of a newly released evolutionary impulse. The spiritual guide functions both as a repository and a transmitter of evolutionary energies. Rome can benefit from the presence of this spiritual "king" only if Romans are capable of recognizing his role and his functionality.

At the conclusion of "Coriolanus", Rome has not yet developed a properly functioning intellect faculty. Rome's overall functionality has been further distracted by the lack of a properly functioning heart faculty and by the presence of a corrupted self faculty. In such a state, Rome is not ready to respond constructively to the presence of the spiritual king. This is illustrated by the inability of the Romans to recognize and accept Julius Caesar's role and functionality. In other words, Julius Caesar's role is incomprehensible to those who are around him. Romans are not familiar, as yet, with the concept and the role of the spiritual king. Therefore their reactions are very different from those described, for example, in the History Plays. Let's recall that the leading aspects of England described in the History Plays do not have a problem with accepting the concept of "king". Their main difficulty is how to recognize *who* is or *who* should be treated as the king. It should be emphasized that England, as described in the History Plays, represents a being on a higher turn of the evolutionary spiral. At that time conscious energy was fully adsorbed. Hence England's overall functionality was much more advanced.

The Romans are not capable of comprehending the need for a king. Based on their experiences from the past, they associate the concept of king with its ordinary and corrupted form. For them king means tyranny, therefore king is the enemy of the people. The king should not be allowed to exercise power; quite the contrary, he should be eliminated to preserve the welfare of the republic.

The readers may notice that 1st century BC Rome closely resembles the being described in "Coriolanus". Brutus and Cassius in "Julius Caesar" represent aspects of an underdeveloped and corrupted intellect faculty. Brutus is a high-ranking and well-regarded Roman nobleman. Brutus represents the leading aspect of the intellect faculty. This is still an underdeveloped aspect that is entirely driven by self-importance. Even though he loves and admires Caesar personally, Brutus participates in the conspiracy to assassinate him. Brutus apparently places the good of Rome above his own personal interests or feelings. In reality, Brutus is rather a naively arrogant man who thinks that he is capable of knowing what is good for Rome:

> "If it be aught toward the general good,
> Set honour in one eye and death i' the other,
> And I will look on both indifferently,
> For let the gods so speed me as I love
> The name of honour more than I fear death."
>
> ...
>
> "It must be by his death: and for my part,
> I know no personal cause to spurn at him,
> But for the general. He would be crown'd."
>
> ...
>
> "If there be any in this assembly, any dear friend of
> Caesar's, to him I say, that Brutus' love to Caesar
> was no less than his. If then that friend demand
> why Brutus rose against Caesar, this is my answer:
> - Not that I loved Caesar less, but that I loved
> Rome more."

The readers may recognize in this character traces of the previous Brutus, a tribune from "Coriolanus". In "Julius Caesar" Brutus' influence has further increased: now he is a senator. Brutus seems to be paranoid about his sense of honour to the extent of becoming gullible. Brutus' gullibility makes him an easy target for Cassius, the "whisperer".

Cassius is a talented general and long-time acquaintance of Caesar. Cassius resents the fact that the Roman populace has come to revere Caesar almost as a god. He slyly leads Brutus to believe that Caesar has become too powerful and must die. He manages to convert Brutus to his cause by sending him forged letters claiming that the Romans support the death of Caesar. A shrewd opportunist, Cassius harbours no illusions about his own intention and his role as the whisperer:

> "Well, Brutus, thou art noble; yet, I see,
> Thy honourable metal may be wrought
> From that it is disposed: therefore it is meet
> That noble minds keep ever with their likes;
> For who so firm that cannot be seduced?
> Caesar doth bear me hard; but he loves Brutus:
> If I were Brutus now and he were Cassius,
> He should not humour me."

Antony represents a partially purified aspect of the heart faculty. He is a loyal friend of Caesar. Antony is impulsive and pleasure seeking, passionate rather than principled. He is extremely spontaneous. The audience may recognize in Antony some traces of Herculean power but in a much more astute form than that demonstrated by Caius Martius in "Coriolanus". The character of Antony clearly indicates a subtle change that the being of Rome has already gone through as a result of the presence of Julius Caesar.

The presence of Julius Caesar also re-activates the previously released conscious and creative energies. The heroines of "Julius Caesar", Calphurnia and Portia, represent impulses of these previously released evolutionary energies. These two elements are still weak but able to exercise their influence, at least partially.

Calphurnia is Julius Caesar's wife. She represents an element of creative energy. She is a spiritual heir of Virgilia from "Coriolanus".

Portia represents an element of conscious energy:

> "I have a man's mind, but a woman's might.
> How hard it is for women to keep counsel!"

She is Brutus' wife. Portia is conscious of the damaging influence of Cassius on her husband. She tries to warn Brutus. However, Brutus arrogantly disregards her warning.

The impulse of unitive energy remains dormant. This impulse cannot be activated as long as Rome is not correctly prepared for it. Shakespeare uses Octavia to symbolically represent this impulse. This is why Octavia does not appear in the play. Octavia is the sister of Octavius, the adopted son of Julius Caesar. Octavia appears in "Antony and Cleopatra", i.e., in the third play of Shakespeare's Roman tetralogy.

Spiritual king

Shakespeare has chosen an interesting way to describe the impact of the spiritual king on Rome. Firstly, the impact is illustrated by the various reactions of the leading aspects of this being toward the possibility of having a "king". Secondly, Shakespeare introduces a series of unusual events and characters that have been missing in "Coriolanus", i.e., soothsayers, violent weather, a variety of bad omens and portents. Shakespeare uses such signs to mark an unfulfilled forceful occasion.

Julius Caesar is presented as the most influential person but he is not the main character of the play. (The character of Caesar appears only in three scenes and is murdered at the exact centre of the play). Nevertheless his presence is so strong that it impacts every other character of the play. This preoccupation with Caesar is triggered by the possibility that he may become king. For noblemen like Brutus and Cassius, who consider themselves equal to Julius Caesar, the coronation of Julius Caesar would mean that they themselves would no longer be free men but would become slaves. This is clearly marked by Cassius' comments to Brutus and Casca:

> "What should be in that 'Caesar'?
> Why should that name be sounded more than yours?
> Write them together, yours is as fair a name;
> Sound them, it doth become the mouth as well;
> Weigh them, it is as heavy; conjure with 'em,
> Brutus will start a spirit as soon as Caesar.
> Now, in the names of all the gods at once,
> Upon what meat doth this our Caesar feed,
> That he is grown so great?"
>
> ...
>
> "And we are govern'd with our mothers' spirits;
> Our yoke and sufferance show us womanish."

It should be emphasized that Caesar never explicitly says that he is the king. Quite the contrary, he refuses the crown in a dramatic public display. Casca describes this event in the following way:

> "I saw Mark
> Antony offer him a crown; - yet 'twas not a crown
> neither, 'twas one of these coronets; - and, as I told
> you, he put it by once ...
>
> Then he
> offered it to him again; then he put it by again ...
>
> And then he offered it the third
> time; he put it the third time by."

Moreover, on several occasions Caesar makes sure that his companions should realize that he is a mortal creature. Therefore he has instigated situations in which he has demonstrated his bodily limitations. For example, Cassius recalls a couple of incidents that have clearly demonstrated Caesar's physical weaknesses. In the first incident Caesar nearly drowned when he challenged Cassius to jump into a cold river:

"For once, upon a raw and gusty day,
The troubled Tiber chafing with her shores,
Caesar said to me 'Darest thou, Cassius, now
Leap in with me into this angry flood,
And swim to yonder point?' Upon the word,
Accoutred as I was, I plunged in
And bade him follow; so indeed he did.
The torrent roar'd, and we did buffet it
With lusty sinews, throwing it aside
And stemming it with hearts of controversy;
But ere we could arrive the point proposed,
Caesar cried 'Help me, Cassius, or I sink!'
I, as Aeneas, our great ancestor,
Did from the flames of Troy upon his shoulder
The old Anchises bear, so from the waves of Tiber
Did I the tired Caesar."

The second incident took place in Spain. At that time Caesar got very sick:

"He had a fever when he was in Spain,
And when the fit was on him, I did mark
How he did shake: 'tis true, this god did shake;
His coward lips did from their colour fly,
And that same eye whose bend doth awe the world
Did lose his lustre: I did hear him groan:
Ay, and that tongue of his that bade the Romans
Mark him and write his speeches in their books,
Alas, it cried 'Give me some drink, Titinius,'
As a sick girl."

Then, while talking to Antony, Caesar indicates that he is hearing-impaired:

"Come on my right hand, for this ear is deaf,
And tell me truly what thou think'st of him."

At the same time, however, Caesar says things that point out that he is special and superior to other mortals. In his own words he refers to himself as "the northern star":

"But I am constant as the northern star,
Of whose true-fix'd and resting quality
There is no fellow in the firmament.
The skies are painted with unnumber'd sparks,
They are all fire and every one doth shine,
But there's but one in all doth hold his place:
So in the world; 'tis furnish'd well with men,
And men are flesh and blood, and apprehensive;
Yet in the number I do know but one
That unassailable holds on his rank,
Unshaked of motion: and that I am he,
Let me a little show it, even in this."

Shakespeare, by comparing Caesar to the northern star, clearly defines his position within the spiritual hierarchy. The northern star is unique in its fixedness. It is the only star that never changes its position in the sky. It is the star by which sailors have navigated since ancient times; it is the star that guides them in their voyages. Such a description corresponds to a highly developed man. This would correspond to an individual whose faculties have been purified, unified, and transmuted. It is in this context that "Caesar" may be regarded as the spiritual king.

Rejection

The current status of Rome is such that this being is incapable of absorbing constructively the newly released impulse of evolutionary energy. Such incapability is further indicated in the episode in which Caesar asks some priests to carry out an animal sacrifice to find out what the current status of Rome is. The priests perform the sacrifice and they find out that:

"Plucking the entrails of an offering forth,
They could not find a heart within the beast."

In other words, Rome is like a beast without a spiritual "heart". The Roman heart is still "barren". Shakespeare inserts another episode that further clarifies the current spiritual state of Rome. In this episode, Caesar asks Antony to "touch" Calphurnia when running in the race:

> "Forget not, in your speed, Antonius,
> To touch Calpurnia; for our elders say,
> The barren, touched in this holy chase,
> Shake off their sterile curse."

In its inner content, "the barren" does not apply to Calphurnia. "The barren" means the Roman heart. Antony represents an aspect of this faculty. Caesar points out that Antony might be awakened through a "touch" of creativity. Calphurnia symbolizes an element of creative energy. While taking part in "this holy chase", Antony might be able to "shake off their sterile curse" from the Roman heart by absorbing creative energy.

However, Rome, as a whole, is not ready for exposure to unitive energy. Unitive energy was transmitted onto humankind but it could not yet be activated. Caesar's assassination symbolically represents Rome's rejection of unitive energy.

The pivotal moment indicating the incapacity of Rome to constructively absorb unitive energy is when Brutus decides to join the assassins. Brutus' decision is critical. If Brutus, who represents the leading aspect of the intellect faculty, is not capable of comprehending the situation, then there is not enough capacity within Rome to fulfill this evolutionary forceful occasion.

Shakespeare dramatically plays out Brutus' decision. He emphasizes its importance by employing a symbolism that he also uses in other plays. At the moment when Brutus becomes converted by Cassius, Caesar has an attack of epilepsy. Here is Casca's report about Caesar's falling sickness:

> "He fell down in the market-place, and foamed at
> mouth, and was speechless."

Shakespeare uses such episodes to mark a critical moment of the evolutionary process. Brutus' decision to join the assassins is such a moment. This particular episode, however, marks a failure: the spiritually pregnable occasion cannot be fulfilled.

Of course Caesar is aware of the coming assassination:

> "What can be avoided
> Whose end is purposed by the mighty gods?
> Yet Caesar shall go forth; for these predictions
> Are to the world in general as to Caesar."

Caesar knows that Cassius is the main instigator of Rome's rejection of the evolutionary opportunity. Right after the epilepsy episode, Caesar warns Antony about Cassius:

> "Would he were fatter! But I fear him not:
> Yet if my name were liable to fear,
> I do not know the man I should avoid
> So soon as that spare Cassius. He reads much;
> He is a great observer and he looks
> Quite through the deeds of men: he loves no plays,
> As thou dost, Antony; he hears no music;
> Seldom he smiles, and smiles in such a sort
> As if he mock'd himself and scorn'd his spirit
> That could be moved to smile at any thing.
> Such men as he be never at heart's ease
> Whiles they behold a greater than themselves,
> And therefore are they very dangerous.
> I rather tell thee what is to be fear'd
> Than what I fear; for always I am Caesar."

In this comment Caesar identifies the main cause of Rome's failure: the presence of Cassius, the whisperer. As long as the whisperer is there and is able to exercise his influence, Rome is incapable of benefiting from the forceful occasion.

Caesar is also trying to alert all those around him about the coming assassination. He makes sure that everybody hears the soothsayer's warning:

Caesar:
"Who is it in the press that calls on me?
I hear a tongue, shriller than all the music,
Cry 'Caesar!' Speak; Caesar is turn'd to hear."

Soothsayer:
"Beware the ides of March."

Caesar also knows that Brutus is one of the assassins. When he sees the assassins coming to his house he welcomes them sarcastically:

"Welcome, Publius.
What, Brutus, are you stirr'd so early too?
Good morrow, Casca. Caius Ligarius,
Caesar was ne'er so much your enemy
As that same ague which hath made you lean."

"I thank you for your pains and courtesy."

"Good friends, go in, and taste some wine with me;
And we, like friends, will straightway go together."

Caesar's welcoming words addressed to Brutus on that morning ("you ... too") are nearly the same as his very last and now very famous phrase that is widely used in Western literature as an epitome of betrayal:

"Et tu, Brute!"

and Shakespeare has him add:

"Then fall, Caesar."

In other words, if Brutus is not able to comprehend the evolutionary opportunity offered to Rome, then there is no need for Caesar there. The assassination of Caesar is a serious failure that impinges on the cosmic plan:

"... and the state of man,
Like to a little kingdom, suffers then

The nature of an insurrection."

Such a rejection is allowed by the measure of freewill that Rome has and its consequences may not be annulled by *force majeure*, no matter how much is at stake. Nevertheless, this rejection disturbs higher-level forces. This is the reason why Rome is plagued with violent weather and a variety of bad omens and portents, the walking dead, and lions stalking through the city. Horatio in "Hamlet" gives a vivid description of this very night:

> "In the most high and palmy state of Rome,
> A little ere the mightiest Julius fell,
> The graves stood tenantless and the sheeted dead
> Did squeak and gibber in the Roman streets:
> As stars with trains of fire and dews of blood,
> Disasters in the sun; and the moist star
> Upon whose influence Neptune's empire stands
> Was sick almost to doomsday with eclipse."

Calphurnia, Caesar's wife, is able to understand the meaning of these unusual events:

> "When beggars die, there are no comets seen;
> The heavens themselves blaze forth the death of princes."

Calphurnia perceives the perfection of Caesar. This is marked by her dream in which she saw a statue of Caesar:

> "Calpurnia here, my wife, stays me at home:
> She dreamt to-night she saw my statua,
> Which, like a fountain with an hundred spouts,
> Did run pure blood: and many lusty Romans
> Came smiling, and did bathe their hands in it."

As mentioned earlier, the number "one hundred" indicates the completion of the ninety nine states of purification. Therefore, "a hundred holes in it, like a fountain" symbolically indicates the degree of Caesar's spiritual perfection. Ironically, it is Decius, one of the conspirators, who is able to perceive the symbolism of

Calphurnia's dream. Decius seemingly convinces Caesar that Calphurnia misinterpreted her dire nightmare and, in fact, no danger awaits him at the Senate:

> "This dream is all amiss interpreted;
> It was a vision fair and fortunate:
> Your statue spouting blood in many pipes,
> In which so many smiling Romans bathed,
> Signifies that from you great Rome shall suck
> Reviving blood, and that great men shall press
> For tinctures, stains, relics and cognizance.
> This by Calpurnia's dream is signified."

And Caesar adds:

> "And this way have you well expounded it."

Because the current status of Rome is such that it is incapable of making constructive use of unitive energy, the process has to be postponed. It has to be delayed for some future time when the being will be ready to benefit from this advanced evolutionary energy. This is illustrated in Calphurnia's dream by Caesar's future statue spouting streams of "sustaining blood".

The reaction of these various aspects clearly demonstrates that they are not ready yet to benefit from the gift that Rome has been endowed with. The assassination of Julius Caesar symbolically represents the rejection of unitive energy. In Antony's word it was the fall that affected all:

> " ... great Caesar fell.
> O, what a fall was there, my countrymen!
> Then I, and you, and all of us fell down."

Therefore, a contingency plan has to be implemented to secure, at least partially, developmental gains from this particular forceful occasion. The implementation of such a contingency plan is the subject of the second part of the play.

Contingency

The contingency plan is specified in Caesar's will. The will consists of two parts.

The first part provides temporary measures. The second part of the will addresses a permanent provision for the future.

<u>Temporary measures</u>
After the assassination Antony reads Caesar's will. The first part of the will bequeaths a sum of money to every citizen:

> "Here is the will, and under Caesar's seal.
> To every Roman citizen he gives,
> To every several man, seventy-five drachmas."

This part of Caesar's will indicates that every citizen of Rome has benefited equally from the presence of Caesar. (The seventy-five drachmas was not a negligible amount at that time; the daily wage of a skilled worker was in the range of one drachma). Technically, this provisional action aims at the reformation of Rome. The reformation may be realized by eliminating the most corruptive aspects and establishing an inner structure that will allow for the constructive use of unitive energy. The elimination of the corruptive aspects is instigated by launching a war against Brutus and Cassius. Antony uses part of the above-mentioned money to finance the war. The "war" in Shakespeare's plays refers to the reformation process.

The reformation aims at aligning the manifest faculties according to a developmental triad. This triad is a earthly projection of its higher heavenly form. The developmental triad is symbolically illustrated by a three-person coalition known as the triumvirate. The triumvirate provides the basic arrangement that allows for efficient absorption of evolutionary energies.

An ancient parable may be used to explain the triad's functionality. In this parable the triad is compared to a chariot. A driver is seated in a chariot that is propelled by a horse. The chariot represents the self faculty; the outward form which allows the driver to move toward its objective. The horse, which is the motive power that allows for an intention to be actualized and a particular action to be carried out, represents the heart faculty. The charioteer represents the intellect faculty. It is this faculty which in a superior manner perceives the purpose and possibility of the situation and makes possible for the chariot to move forward and gain its objective. One of the three, on its own, will be able to fulfill its function. However, the combined function of reaching its destination cannot be realized unless all three faculties are aligned in the right way.

The readers will recognize that the parable explains the functionality of correctly aligned manifest faculties. Such an alignment has been previously described as consisting of two forms of control, i.e., where the intellect controls the heart and the heart controls the self. Shakespeare uses the historical triumvirate to illustrate the functionality of the developmental triad.

Octavius is Caesar's adopted son and his spiritual successor. He arrives on the scene immediately after Caesar's death. Octavius represents a highly developed aspect of the intellect faculty. It is this aspect that was visibly missing at the time of "Coriolanus". In other words, the appearance of Octavius is another derivative effect of the presence of Julius Caesar. Upon his arrival in Rome, Octavius forms a triumvirate with Antony and Lepidus. Octavius plays the role of the charioteer. His role is to prepare the developmental triad that will allow the absorption of the impulse of unitive energy, which activation had to be delayed. Because of his advanced state, Octavius himself is able to absorb a fraction of the impulse. Shakespeare quite precisely, even quantitatively, defined the portion of unitive energy that Octavius is capable of absorbing. This is spelled out in Octavius' comment:

> "Look;
> I draw a sword against conspirators;
> When think you that the sword goes up again?
> Never, till Caesar's three and thirty wounds
> Be well avenged; or till another Caesar
> Have added slaughter to the sword of traitors."

The number "three and thirty wounds" symbolically corresponds to one third of the total ninety nine purification states. This means that, at this very moment, Octavius is incapable of handling the entire impulse. He is able to absorb one third of the total charge. The triumvirate has to be formed so the impulse could be fully utilized by Rome. Otherwise the spiritual "wine", which symbolically represents the effect of the exposure to unitive energy, cannot be correctly digested.

Antony represents an aspect of the heart faculty. After the death of Julius Caesar he starts to demonstrate some intuitive skills. Here is his prediction given over Caesar's dead body:

> "Domestic fury and fierce civil strife
> Shall cumber all the parts of Italy;
> Blood and destruction shall be so in use
> And dreadful objects so familiar
> That mothers shall but smile when they behold
> Their infants quarter'd with the hands of war;
> All pity choked with custom of fell deeds:
> And Caesar's spirit, ranging for revenge,
> With Ate by his side come hot from hell,
> Shall in these confines with a monarch's voice
> Cry 'Havoc,' and let slip the dogs of war;
> That this foul deed shall smell above the earth
> With carrion men, groaning for burial."

Antony's prediction applies to the entire cycle that is described by Shakespeare in the Roman tetralogy. The final actualization of Antony's prediction is illustrated in "Titus Andronicus".

Antony, however, is not able to understand the overall function of the newly formed triad. He attempts to corrupt the triad by trying to control Octavius. The readers may recognize in Antony's behaviour some echo of Volumnia's character from "Coriolanus". This is clearly marked on several occasions. For example, Antony is getting impatient with Octavius who ignores his recommendations and instead follows his own:

> Antony to Octavius:
> "Why do you cross me in this exigent?"

Octavius:
"I do not cross you; but I will do so."

And then, during the battle at Philippi, Octavius tells Antony:

"Now, Antony, our hopes are answered:
You said the enemy would not come down,
But keep the hills and upper regions;
It proves not so: their battles are at hand;
They mean to warn us at Philippi here,
Answering before we do demand of them."

Antony entirely misjudges the importance of Lepidus to the proper functioning of the triumvirate:

"This is a slight unmeritable man,
Meet to be sent on errands: is it fit,
The three-fold world divided, he should stand
One of the three to share it?"

Lepidus represents an aspect of the reformed self faculty. He is a crucial component of the triumvirate.

Antony's behaviour is a sign of the reoccurrence of the tendencies that appeared at the time of "Coriolanus". In other words, Antony's behaviour is a reflection of inner inadequacies that were previously manifested by Volumnia and Caius Martius. These inadequacies will again come into the open sometimes later on. They are described in "Antony and Cleopatra".

Permanent provision for the future
The second part of the contingency plan addresses a provision for the future developmental needs. This is symbolically specified in the second part of Julius Caesar's will:

"Moreover, he hath left you all his walks,
His private arbours and new-planted orchards,
On this side Tiber; he hath left them you,
And to your heirs for ever, common pleasures,

To walk abroad, and recreate yourselves.
Here was a Caesar! when comes such another?"

By including Caesar's private "garden" in his will, Shakespeare makes a reference to an access to higher states of mind. Such an access was made available to mankind as a result of the release of unitive energy. Before that time, man was disconnected from this "garden".

The "garden" is placed "on this side of the Tiber River", which means that it is accessible in this world. Caesar's will emphasizes the fact that the garden has been left "to you and to your heirs forever". In other words, the appearance of Caesar has provided mankind with a permanent potentiality of accessing higher states of mind. Calphurnia saw in her dream such a garden that "will provide great Rome with sustaining blood". Another important feature is that the garden is made public: the access to the garden is not restricted to a selected group of people, a culture, or a country.

The play "Julius Caesar" provides further indications about the forces associated with the higher states. These forces are used to eliminate the corrupted aspects of Rome. This is in accordance with the rules that govern the reformation process. Namely, one of the rules requires that these aspects that have not fulfilled their developmental potential should be partially purified before they are eliminated. Brutus is subjected to such a process. Brutus perceives the presence of invisible forces as a sort of "tidal movement". This is very similar to Joan of Arc's experience described in "Henry VI". Here is Brutus' remark about it:

"There is a tide in the affairs of men,
Which, taken at the flood, leads on to fortune;
Omitted, all the voyage of their life
Is bound in shallows and in miseries.
On such a full sea are we now afloat;
And we must take the current when it serves,
Or lose our ventures."

Brutus is convinced that it is the right time to begin a battle against Octavius and Antony. He believes that if he and Cassius do not seize "a tide" now, i.e., when the time is right, they will lose their opportunity. Brutus does not realize that he, similarly to Joan of Arc, has already missed his chance. His greatest chance ever was his friendship with Caesar. Brutus repeatedly fails to interpret correctly situations and opportunities that are offered to him.

Before the battle against Octavius Caesar and Mark Antony, Brutus finds out that Portia, his wife, has committed suicide. This symbolically indicates that Brutus' evolutionary potentiality has been completely lost. Brutus still does not realize the importance of Portia's death. But Cassius does:

"O insupportable and touching loss!"

The death of Portia is followed by the appearance of Caesar's ghost. When Brutus sees the ghost he is terrified:

"Art thou any thing?
Art thou some god, some angel, or some devil,
That makest my blood cold and my hair to stare?
Speak to me what thou art."

And the ghost explains:

"Thy evil spirit, Brutus."

Previously Brutus ignored Portia's warning. Now the ghost informs him that his time has run out:

"To tell thee thou shalt see me at Philippi."

The ghost is an evil spirit appearing to Brutus' eyes only. The ghost is not so much the cause of the corruption of the being. It is a reflection of this already corrupted aspect that is represented by Brutus. The ghost represents Brutus' own corrupted inner state. The ghost foretells Brutus' death at Philippi; then Brutus will meet his own corrupted soul.

Later on, when the ghost of Caesar reappears on the battlefield at Philippi, Brutus finally starts to understand his situation. He courageously accepts his defeat and the inevitability of his failure:

> "O Julius Caesar, thou art mighty yet!
> Thy spirit walks abroad and turns our swords
> In our own proper entrails."

Cassius, the principal architect of the assassination, also goes through a similar realization. At one point he starts to perceive what awaits him in the near future:

> "You know that I held Epicurus strong
> And his opinion: now I change my mind,
> And partly credit things that do presage.
> Coming from Sardis, on our former ensign
> Two mighty eagles fell, and there they perch'd,
> Gorging and feeding from our soldiers' hands;
> Who to Philippi here consorted us:
> This morning are they fled away and gone;
> And in their steads do ravens, crows and kites,
> Fly o'er our heads and downward look on us,
> As we were sickly prey: their shadows seem
> A canopy most fatal, under which
> Our army lies, ready to give up the ghost."

Cassius dies proclaiming that Caesar is avenged:

> "Now be a freeman: and with this good sword,
> That ran through Caesar's bowels, search this bosom.
> Stand not to answer: here, take thou the hilts;
> And, when my face is cover'd, as 'tis now,
> Guide thou the sword."
>
> ...
>
> "Caesar, thou art revenged,
> Even with the sword that kill'd thee."

Shakespeare uses Messala and Titinius, Cassius' friends, to deliver the final comments on Cassius' and, by extension, on Brutus' death. They both died because they failed to perceive the truth:

> "O error, soon conceived,

Thou never comest unto a happy birth,
But kill'st the mother that engender'd thee!"

...

"Alas, thou hast misconstrued every thing!"

The most corrupted aspects of Rome are eliminated. Only now Rome is ready for the postponed exposure to unitive energy.

Conclusion

At the time of "Julius Caesar" unitive energy was made available to mankind. However, Julius Caesar's assassination did not allow for its accommodation. Ironically, it is Cassius who gives the best summary of the Roman failure. Here is Cassius' sarcastic, nevertheless accurate, pronouncement on the significance of Caesar's assassination:

"How many ages hence
Shall this our lofty scene be acted over
In states unborn and accents yet unknown!"

Shakespeare has used the historical character of Julius Caesar to describe the effect of switching on unitive energy. This was an event of great importance in the evolutionary history of mankind. The effect of this event is everlasting, similarly to the historical importance of Julius Caesar. Julius Caesar has instilled in the Romans a desire to replace the old republic with a monarchy. At the same time the concept of "Caesar" was imprinted onto human consciousness. During the play the name "Caesar" underwent a metamorphosis, from an individual man's name to the title of an institution. The word "Caesar" then became a synonym for "Emperor".

Similarly, the spiritual potentiality of Rome was gradually transmuted from a lower evolutionary stage, as described in "Coriolanus", to a more advanced one after its preliminary exposure to unitive energy. Although this event was only partially utilized at the time of "Antony and Cleopatra", it affected countries that didn't even exist at that time.

2.3 Awakening in "Antony and Cleopatra"

Introduction

Similarly to "Coriolanus" and "Julius Caesar", the direct source for "Antony and Cleopatra" was Sir Thomas North's translation of Plutarch's "Lives of the Noble Greeks and Romans". A large number of phrases within Shakespeare's play are taken directly from North's prose. As in the other plays, Shakespeare adds several scenes and often adjusts historical facts to accommodate them to his presentation of the evolutionary process.

"Antony and Cleopatra" describes the continuation of the process that has been initiated at the time of "Julius Caesar". In "Julius Caesar" Shakespeare portrays Rome when it is not ready yet for the experience associated with the exposure to unitive energy. Therefore, the triumvirate is formed as a measure to allow Rome to absorb unitive energy. The triumvirate acts as a triad that the inner being may acquire and then gradually can integrate within itself. This triad may be emulated by other beings that happen to come into contact with it. In this way a group of people, a country, or an entire culture may absorb an evolutionary impulse and be transformed by it.

"Antony and Cleopatra" presents the outcome of the exposure of Rome to unitive energy at the time of Octavius Caesar.

Historical background

Marcus Antonius (83 - 30 BC), known in English as Mark Antony, was a Roman politician and general. He was a supporter of Julius Caesar as a military commander and administrator. After Caesar's assassination, Mark Antony was a member of a political alliance with Octavius Caesar and Lepidus. The alliance is known today as the Second Triumvirate. The Second Triumvirate was formed on November 26th, 43 BC.

Octavius was adopted by Julius Caesar, who was his great uncle, and came into his inheritance after Caesar's assassination in 44 BC. Octavius was 19 years old at that time.

The triumvirate broke up in 33 BC. Disagreement between Octavius Caesar and Mark Antony erupted into civil war in 31 BC. Mark Antony was defeated by Octavius Caesar at the naval Battle of Actium, and in a brief land battle at Alexandria. He committed suicide, and his lover, Queen Cleopatra VII of Egypt, killed herself shortly thereafter.

Octavius Caesar was the first emperor of the Roman Empire, who ruled from 27 BC until his death in 14 AD.

Storyline

Mark Antony, one of the triumvirs of the Roman Empire, spends his time in Egypt, living a life of decadence and having an affair with the country's beautiful queen, Cleopatra. In Mark Antony's absence, Octavius Caesar and Lepidus, his fellow triumvirs, worry about the increasing strength of Pompey, their archrival. Octavius Caesar is upset at Mark Antony for neglecting his duties as a statesman and military officer in order to live a decadent life by Cleopatra's side. Mark Antony decides to return to Rome when a message arrives informing him that his wife, Fulvia, is dead and that Pompey is raising an army to rebel against the triumvirate.

Realizing that an alliance is necessary to defeat Pompey, Mark Antony and Octavius Caesar agree that Mark Antony will marry Octavius' sister, Octavia, which will solidify their loyalty to one another. Enobarbus, Mark Antony's closest friend, predicts that despite the marriage Mark Antony will surely return to Cleopatra.

In Egypt, Cleopatra flies into a jealous rage when she learns of Mark Antony's marriage. However, when a messenger delivers word that Octavia is plain and unimpressive, Cleopatra becomes confident that she will win Mark Antony back.

The triumvirs meet Pompey and settle their differences without going to battle. Pompey agrees to keep peace in exchange for rule over Sicily and Sardinia. That evening, the men drink to celebrate their truce.

Mark Antony and Octavia depart for Athens. Once they are gone, Octavius Caesar breaks the truce, wages war against Pompey, and defeats him. After using Lepidus' army to secure the victory, he accuses Lepidus of treason, imprisons him, and confiscates his land and possessions. This news angers Mark Antony, as do the rumours that Octavius Caesar has been speaking out against him in public. Octavia pleads with Mark Antony to maintain a peaceful relationship with her brother. Should Mark Antony and Octavius Caesar fight, she says, her affections would be painfully divided. Mark Antony dispatches her to Rome on a peace mission, and quickly returns to Cleopatra. There he raises an army to fight Octavius Caesar. Octavius Caesar commands his army and navy to Egypt. Mark Antony, ignoring all advice to the contrary, elects to fight him at sea, allowing Cleopatra to command a ship. Mark Antony's forces lose the battle when Cleopatra's ship flees and Mark Antony's follows, leaving the rest of the fleet vulnerable.

Mark Antony despairs, condemning Cleopatra for having led him into infamy but quickly forgiving her. He and Cleopatra send requests to their conqueror: Mark Antony asks to be allowed to live in Egypt, while Cleopatra asks that her kingdom be passed down to her rightful heirs. Octavius Caesar dismisses Mark Antony's request, but he promises Cleopatra a fair hearing if she betrays her lover. Cleopatra seems to be giving thought to Octavius Caesar's message when Mark Antony barges in and curses her for her treachery.

Mark Antony meets Octavius Caesar's troops in a land battle and scores an unexpected victory. Another day brings another battle, and once again Mark Antony meets Octavius Caesar at sea. As before, the Egyptian fleet proves treacherous; it abandons the fight and leaves Mark Antony to suffer defeat. Convinced that his lover has betrayed him, Mark Antony vows to kill Cleopatra. In order to protect herself, she quarters herself in her monument and sends word that she has committed suicide.

Mark Antony, racked with grief, determines to join his queen in the afterlife. He commands one of his attendants to fulfill his promise of unquestioned service and kill him. The attendant kills himself instead. Mark Antony then falls on his own sword, but the wound is not immediately fatal. He is carried to Cleopatra's monument, where the lovers are reunited briefly before Mark Antony's death.

Octavius Caesar takes the queen prisoner, planning to display her in Rome as a testament to the might of his empire, but she learns of his plan and kills herself with the help of poisonous snakes. Octavius Caesar has her buried beside Mark Antony.

Meeting of the triumvirs

The triumvirate represents the lower (earthly) triad of the evolutionary transmission chain. Octavius Caesar acts as the leading and guiding aspect. Lepidus represents an aspect of the self faculty. Mark Antony illustrates a partially purified but unreformed aspect of the heart. Through Calphurnia's "touch" in "Julius Caesar", Mark Antony has been exposed to creative energy. However, his encounter with Cleopatra has somewhat diminished the effect of this exposure. This is symbolically marked in the play by the death of Fulvia, Mark Antony's wife.

By absorbing an element of unitive energy, the lower triad can be transformed into an intermediary triad of the evolutionary transmission chain. An intermediary triad is characterized by some degree of spiritual mobility; it allows the earthly triad to reach an intermediary inspirational state. Such a transition from an earthly to an intermediary triad is referred to as "passing through water".

The intermediary triad structure consists of (i) an advanced (purified) aspect, (ii) an impulse of unitive energy, and (iii) a reformed aspect of the being. In this particular case the intermediary triad may be formed by bringing together Octavius Caesar, Octavia, and Mark Antony. Octavius Caesar initiates and directs the preparation for such a triad. The first step of the preparation requires Mark Antony to marry Octavia. Octavia, Octavius' sister, represents the deferred element of unitive energy.

The marriage provides the needed structure for the constructive absorption of unitive energy. In Octavius' words, Octavia is "a great part of myself":

> "You take from me a great part of myself;
> Use me well in 't. Sister, prove such a wife
> As my thoughts make thee, and as my farthest band
> Shall pass on thy approof."

Unitive energy acts as unifying force. This is why Octavius Caesar says that the marriage will serve to "knit their hearts with an unslipping knot". The marriage of Mark Antony and Octavia is followed by a wine drinking party. The effect of unitive energy is manifested during the triumvirs' party.

It is significant that the wine drinking party takes place on board of Pompey's galley. An island represents an intermediary inspirational state. Such an intermediary state may be reached by "passing through water". The triad is a vehicle that allows to make such a journey. The fact that the triumvirs' meeting takes place on a galley, or a "temporary island", points out that this particular state is not permanent yet. Nevertheless, it is then and there that the triumvirs are exposed to an impact of unitive energy.

The effect of "wine drinking" symbolically illustrates the capacity of the triumvirs to effectively absorb unitive energy.

Lepidus gets drunk during the party. Lepidus' developmental state is such that he is not able to withstand the impact of unitive energy. He is not part of the intermediary triad. Therefore, he has to go. Indeed, Lepidus makes only one more appearance before being eliminated by Octavius Caesar.

Mark Antony is also having difficulties with the effect of "wine". When Octavius Caesar interrupts the wine drinking festivities to remind Mark Antony that there is more serious business to be done, Mark Antony's answer is the most telling phrase describing his inner state:

> "be a child o'th' time."

Mark Antony tries to persuade Octavius Caesar to forget duty and he urges his men to drink until they reach complete lethargy:

> "Come, let's all take hands,
> Till that the conquering wine hath steep'd our sense
> In soft and delicate Lethe."

In this particular context, "lethargy" indicates spiritual intoxication. The main purpose of the availability of such inspirational states is not their enjoyment but gaining capacity for carrying on additional responsibilities. However, Mark Antony prefers to enjoy the moment. He neglects his duties in order to enjoy his "drunkenness". His tendency to live according to the moment, with little regard for the overall process, is one of the factors of his failure.

After the party Mark Antony abandons Octavia and returns to Egypt. At this point the triad collapses. The impulse of unitive energy is withdrawn from Rome.

Corruption of Mark Antony

As the play progresses, Mark Antony continues to experience conflicting attractions that play out the struggle between his needs and his wants. At one moment, he is the vengeful war hero whom Octavius Caesar praises. Soon thereafter, he sacrifices his military position by unwisely allowing Cleopatra to command a naval ship. Mark Antony likens his shifting self to a cloud that changes shape as it tumbles across the sky. Just as the cloud turns from "a bear or lion, a towered citadel, a pendent rock," so does Mark Antony change from being the renowned conqueror to a victim of Cleopatra's charm:

> "Sometimes we see a cloud that's dragonish;
> A vapour sometime like a bear or lion,
> A tower'd citadel, a pendent rock,
> A forked mountain, or blue promontory
> With trees upon't, that nod unto the world,

And mock our eyes with air: thou hast seen
these signs;
They are black vesper's pageants."

As he says to his attendant, it is difficult for him to "hold this visible shape":

"... here I am Antony:
Yet cannot hold this visible shape, my knave."

The above image may be further explained with the help of the following quote by a 14th century guide who compares experiences that are driven by emotions to "a cloud which for a time seems to have substance, but which a puff of wind will banish to nothingness".

During the night after Mark Antony's sea-battle fiasco, the soldiers on the streets of Alexandria hear music coming from "under the earth":

" 'Tis the god Hercules, whom Antony loved,
Now leaves him."

The departure of Hercules symbolically marks Mark Antony's loss of his evolutionary potential.

The transformation from a lower to an intermediary state is marked by "passing through water". As manifested during the wine drinking party, Mark Antony is not able to sustain such a transition. His current stage allows him to access only the lowest, i.e., an earthly state. This is clearly emphasized by Mark Antony's soldier:

"... we
Have used to conquer, standing on the earth,
And fighting foot to foot."

Nevertheless, Mark Antony arrogantly attempts to fight Octavius Caesar in a sea battle. Here is a compelling description of Mark Antony's sea battle fiasco:

"Antony,
Claps on his sea-wing, and, like a doting mallard,
Leaving the fight in height, flies after her:
I never saw an action of such shame;
Experience, manhood, honour, ne'er before
Did violate so itself."

Mark Antony, by allowing Cleopatra to command the naval ship, symbolically shows that he has allowed himself to be driven by emotions and passions. He cannot "pass through water" as long as he is driven by emotions and passions.

As his Roman allies, even the ever-faithful Enobarbus, abandon him, Mark Antony feels that he has, indeed, lost himself in "dotage", and he determines to rescue his noble identity by taking his own life:

"Betray'd I am:
O this false soul of Egypt! this grave charm."

"Like a right gipsy, hath, at fast and loose,
Beguiled me to the very heart of loss."

Till his last moment Mark Antony remains arrogant and wilful:

"Not Caesar's valour hath o'erthrown Antony,
But Antony's hath triumph'd on itself."

Mark Antony dies believing himself to be a man of honour, discipline, and reason. However, Mark Antony is, in the end, an aspect that has been destroyed by his own weaknesses. It is the basic requirement of the evolutionary process that emotions should be overruled by a higher aim. Whenever emotions veil the overall aim, such a situation always leads to failure. Mark Antony is an undeniable example of such a failure.

Cleopatra's effect

Mark Antony's behaviour illustrates the premature awakening of an inner faculty. Such a premature spiritual experience may lead to excitement and enjoyment, but it forms a barrier against further growth.

Shakespeare describes such an immature experience as the destructive effect that Cleopatra has on Mark Antony. The entire Mark Antony - Cleopatra encounter is a precise description of the experience that ultimately leads to self-destruction. In other words, Shakespeare uses the character of Cleopatra to illustrate a destructive "whisperer". The whisperer's sophistication and degree of deception correspond to the quality and the spiritual state of the being. The more advanced the being, the more sophisticated are the tricks and temptations that are employed by the whisperer. Shakespeare gives a compelling description of such deceptive aims by comparing them to "catching fish". Here are Cleopatra's own words which describe her purpose:

> "Give me mine angle; we'll to the river: there,
> My music playing far off, I will betray
> Tawny-finn'd fishes; my bended hook shall pierce
> Their slimy jaws; and, as I draw them up,
> I'll think them every one an Antony,
> And say 'Ah, ha! You're caught'."

The target of the whisperer is usually the aspect whose corruption would have the greatest destructive impact on the entire process. That's why Mark Antony is Cleopatra's primary catch.

Cleopatra employs a number of approaches to exercise her influence on the selected target. She can be a decadent attractive woman and a ruler at the same time. In the play she is called "salt Cleopatra" and an "enchantress" who has made Mark Antony "the noble ruin of her magic". She is described as a lustful "gipsy," a "wrangling queen", a "slave", an "Egyptian dish", and a "whore". Certainly, all these descriptions have much to do with Cleopatra's beauty and her attractiveness, which, as Enobarbus points out in his description of her, are awe-inspiring:

> "The barge she sat in, like a burnish'd throne,
> Burn'd on the water: the poop was beaten gold;

Purple the sails, and so perfumed that
The winds were love-sick with them; the oars were silver,
Which to the tune of flutes kept stroke, and made
The water which they beat to follow faster,
As amorous of their strokes. For her own person,
It beggar'd all description: she did lie
In her pavilion -cloth-of-gold of tissue -
O'er-picturing that Venus where we see
The fancy outwork nature: on each side her
Stood pretty dimpled boys, like smiling Cupids,
With divers-colour'd fans, whose wind did seem
To glow the delicate cheeks which they did cool,
And what they undid did."

The above description of Cleopatra testifies to her power. It also parallels Joan of Arc's effect described in the History Play, when Joan of Arc makes a reference to this particular scene:

"Now am I like that proud insulting ship
Which Caesar and his fortune bare at once."

Cleopatra is able to use her charm to make "vilest things" appear as things of beauty. Under Cleopatra's influence even priests alter their understanding of what is holy and what is sinful:

"vilest things
Become themselves in her, that the holy priests
Bless her when she is riggish."

By mocking Mark Antony, Cleopatra weakens his relation with Octavius Caesar:

"If the scarce-bearded Caesar have not sent
His powerful mandate to you, 'Do this, or this;
Take in that kingdom, and enfranchise that;
Perform 't, or else we damn thee'."

Her mode of operation is further illustrated by the instructions that she gives her servant whom she sends to spy on Mark Antony:

"See where he is, who's with him, what he does:
I did not send you: if you find him sad,
Say I am dancing; if in mirth, report
That I am sudden sick: quick, and return."

It should be emphasized though that Mark Antony's comprehension was enhanced by his previous exposure to creative energy. This is clearly indicated in the conversation between him and Cleopatra:

Cleopatra:
"If it be love indeed, tell me how much."

Mark Antony:
"There's beggary in the love that can be reckoned."

Cleopatra:
"I'll set a bourn how far to be beloved."

Mark Antony:
"Then must thou needs find out new heaven, new earth."

In the above quote Cleopatra expresses her expectation that love should be declared or demonstrated. She wants to hear and see exactly how much Mark Antony loves her. Cleopatra is talking about ordinary love. However, Mark Antony intuitively realizes that he is faced with not so ordinary a love. Mark Antony compares his previous experience of "drunkenness" to the discovery of "new heaven, new earth", i.e., territory that is unknown to Cleopatra.

Throughout the play Mark Antony grapples with the conflict between his attraction to Cleopatra and his duties to the Roman Empire, between his emotions and his responsibilities. Soon after his nonchalant dismissal of Octavius Caesar's messenger, he chastises himself for his neglect and decides to return to Rome, for fear that he may:

"... lose myself in dotage."

It is not only Cleopatra that mars Mark Antony's awakening. Cleopatra's soothsayer is also tempting Mark Antony. When Mark Antony asks the soothsayer about his fortunes:

> "Whose fortunes shall rise higher, Caesar's or mine?"

The soothsayer answers openly:

> "Caesar's."

Then the soothsayer continues his temping of Mark Antony:

> "Therefore, O Antony, stay not by his side:
> Thy demon, that's thy spirit which keeps thee, is
> Noble, courageous high, unmatchable,
> Where Caesar's is not; but, near him, thy angel
> Becomes a fear, as being o'erpower'd: therefore
> Make space enough between you."

The soothsayer, however, cannot lie. He can only present his message in such a way that it is most attractive to Mark Antony. This is very nicely shown in the above quote. The soothsayer openly tells Mark Antony that it is "thy demon" that drives him right now. In order to let this demon to act as "thy angel", Mark Antony has to separate himself from Octavius Caesar by making "space enough between you". The soothsayer makes clear to Mark Antony that he does not have any chance of winning if he is too close to Caesar:

> "To none but thee; no more, but when to thee.
> If thou dost play with him at any game,
> Thou art sure to lose; and, of that natural luck,
> He beats thee 'gainst the odds: thy lustre thickens,
> When he shines by: I say again, thy spirit
> Is all afraid to govern thee near him;
> But, he away, 'tis noble."

Mark Antony does not understand that he can win only by working harmoniously and obediently under Octavius Caesar's leadership and within the structure of the triad. When the Soothsayer manages to convince Mark Antony about his own greatness, his chances to win are annulled. Mark Antony's selfish tendencies are much stronger than his inner heart's desire. His newly acquired extra-ordinary powers combined with selfish wants lead him astray toward domination, seeking excitements and enjoyment of worldly pleasures. However, his inner heart's desire would require him to become Octavius Caesar's obedient servant. Such an option is beyond Mark Antony's current ability.

Mark Antony twice does battle with Octavius Caesar at sea, and both times his navy is betrayed by Cleopatra's retreat. The fleeing ships are reminders of the inconstancy of the attractions that are represented by Cleopatra. Cleopatra's fleeing ships are a symbol of wavering emotions and changeability of passions. The fleeting Egyptian battle ships illustrate the impotence of false spiritual experiences. They represent a major obstacle in the evolutionary process. No one under the influence of stirred emotions is able to "pass through water" and experience true growth. "Egypt" represents such a false developmental state.

At one point Mark Antony realizes that he has been destroyed by "Egypt":

> "O, whither hast thou led me, Egypt? See,
> How I convey my shame out of thine eyes
> By looking back what I have left behind
> 'story'd in dishonour."

> "Egypt, thou knew'st too well
> My heart was to thy rudder tied by the strings,
> And thou shouldst tow me after …"

> "You did know
> How much you were my conqueror; and that
> My sword, made weak by my affection, would
> Obey it on all cause."

Attraction to "Egypt" is like a phantom. This attraction does not present any real value. It is only a mirage, an abstract, just like

Cleopatra's fearful sails:

> "Forgive my fearful sails! I little thought
> You would have follow'd."

But then Cleopatra's single tear is enough to erase Mark Antony's flashes of realization:

> "Fall not a tear, I say; one of them rates
> All that is won and lost: give me a kiss;
> Even this repays me."

However, Cleopatra and her mission cannot be carried on any longer once her main prey, Mark Antony, is dead:

> "Ah, women, women, look,
> Our lamp is spent, it's out!"

It is then that Cleopatra admits into her presence a Clown. Shakespeare uses Clowns as messengers of cryptic instructions; they appear at the critical moments of the process. The Clown brings a basket with poisonous snakes. Here is Cleopatra's comment about the Clown's appearance:

> "What poor an instrument
> May do a noble deed! he brings me liberty.
> My resolution's placed, and I have nothing
> Of woman in me: now from head to foot
> I am marble-constant; now the fleeting moon
> No planet is of mine."

There is no need for Cleopatra's charm if there is no Mark Antony anymore. There is no need for the "moon" when there is "no planet".

One of the most memorable symbols in the play comes in its final moments when Cleopatra places deadly snakes on her skin. As she lifts one snake, then another to her breast, they become her children and she their wet nurse:

"Dost thou not see my baby at my breast,
That sucks the nurse asleep?"

The snakes represent Cleopatra's nature; her very being is bound to the earth. She is a symbolic representation of the obstacle that holds back man from developmental progress toward a higher aim. Her very nature prevents man from accessing a treasure that traditionally is guarded by a snake. However, Cleopatra's death does not indicate the annihilation of the forces that she represents. Echo of such destructive influences is described in other Shakespeare's plays. "Cleopatra's effect" is always associated with a being that has been exposed to the unitive energy of love without proper preparation. When a being is awakened prematurely, it means that this being is awakened in a wrong way.

Rescue attempts

Despite the fact that Mark Antony is driven away from the right path, Octavius Caesar tries to rescue him on several occasions.

Octavius Caesar's aim is not to eliminate Mark Antony. Before the land battle Octavius Caesar advises his troops to make sure that Mark Antony is not killed:

"Our will is Antony be took alive."

Octavius Caesar's aim is to rescue Mark Antony by bringing him back on the right path, even to the extent of allowing Mark Antony to get a taste of so much desired victory. Indeed, Mark Antony scores an unexpected victory in the land battle. It seems that this victory should have given him another chance to reflect upon his aim, his situation, and his responsibility. During the battle comes another and most striking sign. Scarus, one of Mark Antony's soldiers, shows him the wound that he has received in the engagement. The wound is in the shape of the letter T; but then it changes its shape and becomes the letter H:

"I had a wound here that was like a T,
But now 'tis made an H."

The meaning of this wound may be explained by using the equivalence of numbers and letters. In this equivalence the letters of the alphabet are assigned numerical values. For example, the letter H corresponds to the number eight and represents the "perfect balance", often symbolized by the octagon. The number eight indicates the completion of the seven evolutionary stages, similarly to the number hundred which marks the completion of the ninety nine purification states. The perfect balance means that the inner structure is based on purified and unified inner faculties. Shakespeare has described an example of such inner structure at the end of "As You Like It":

"Here's eight that must take hands

> To join in Hymen's bands,
> If truth holds true contents."

The letter T corresponds to the number nine and stands for inner or secret knowledge, sometimes represented by the enneagon, i.e., nine-pointed figure. The secret knowledge allows to access extraordinary powers. Such extraordinary powers are available to man whose inner faculties have been unified and transmuted in a certain way. The correct developmental sequence, therefore, requires achieving the "perfect balance" as the necessary step leading toward "secret knowledge". This sequence is symbolically indicated as the transition of the letter H into the letter T. The above-quoted scene, however, shows the reverse sequence, i.e., the letter T changes into the letter H. This reverse sequence is used to indicate the danger associated with the attempt of employing secret knowledge (enneagon) before first achieving the inner harmony (octagon). Such cases of prematurely activated powers have been demonstrated by Joan of Arc and Talbot in the History Plays, and by Caius Martius in "Coriolanus". Therefore, the message that is shown to Mark Antony is a warning that he is following the wrong way; his present actions go against the developmental sequence. Mark Antony cannot achieve his goal without being in harmony with Octavius Caesar. The fact that Mark Antony does not understand the message is a further indication that he is already out of touch with the evolutionary process. He ignores the message. Instead, he is overtaken by his apparent triumph:

> "We have beat him to his camp: run one before,
> And let the queen know of our guests. To-morrow,
> Before the sun shall see 's, we'll spill the blood
> That has to-day escaped."

Following the land battle victory, Mark Antony nonchalantly and ignorantly accepts to combat Octavius Caesar in another sea battle:

> "Their preparation is to-day by sea;
> We please them not by land."

> "I would they'ld fight i' the fire or i' the air;

We'ld fight there too."

Mark Antony boasts about being able to fight "in the fire or in the air". As discussed previously, he has not been able to sustain the state of "water"; the higher states of "air" and "fire" are beyond his reach.

At this point the rescue attempts are terminated. Mark Antony's arrogance and ignorance lead him to his ultimate destruction.

Octavius' transformation

In the wine drinking scene Octavius Caesar alone is able to withstand the impact of "drunkenness". Afterwards, Octavius displays extraordinary skills. These extraordinary skills are the sign of the purified aspect that Octavius represents. Here is Mark Antony's comment on Octavius' extraordinary powers:

> "Is it not strange, Canidius,
> That from Tarentum and Brundusium
> He could so quickly cut the Ionian sea,
> And take in Toryne?"

> "Can he be there in person? 'tis impossible;
> Strange that power should be."

And others also notice that:

> "This speed of Caesar's
> Carries beyond belief."

> "While he was yet in Rome,
> His power went out in such distractions as
> Beguiled all spies."

It may be presumed that during the wine drinking party Octavius' state was further elevated. Now he functions as a link to the evolutionary transmission chain.

As the result of Octavius' elevation, his role and his responsibilities have been fulfilled. However, the overall evolutionary potential of Rome has been greatly reduced. As Octavius Caesar explains, the main reason of Rome fiasco was Mark Antony's craving for the place at the "top of all design":

> "we could not stall together
> In the whole world: but yet let me lament,
> With tears as sovereign as the blood of hearts,
> That thou, my brother, my competitor
> In top of all design, my mate in empire,
> Friend and companion in the front of war,
> The arm of mine own body, and the heart
> Where mine his thoughts did kindle ... "

Octavius Caesar sadly refers to Mark Antony as "a moiety of the world". After the wine drinking party the evolutionary triad was disassembled. Before his death Mark Antony was one of two remaining parts of this dismantled structure. This is why Mark Antony's death did not make "a greater crack" and did not "shook lions into civil street" as it was the case after the death of Julius Caesar:

> "The breaking of so great a thing should make
> A greater crack: the round world
> Should have shook lions into civil streets,
> And citizens to their dens: the death of Antony
> Is not a single doom; in the name lay
> A moiety of the world."

After Mark Antony's death there is only one aspect of the triad that is left - Octavius Caesar. Such an arrangement is far from the optimal solution. However, it is the only possible one for the current state of Rome. Octavius Caesar was able to reinstate Rome's link to the transmission chain. But he was not be able to uplift Rome's evolutionary state.

Conclusion

Rome at the time of "Antony and Cleopatra" has temporarily adsorbed some unitive energy, but it is only its intellect faculty that has been uplifted. The other faculties of Rome are still very much at underdeveloped stages. There is a similarity between the Roman plays and the History Plays. Namely, the evolutionary state of Octavius Caesar corresponds to that of Henry V, but on a lower turn of the evolutionary spiral. As the readers will find out, an exposure to the highest evolutionary energy will be needed to pass over the threshold that Rome stumbled upon in its effort toward evolutionary progression.

In the meantime, however, the biggest victory of Octavius Caesar is that which was Cleopatra's biggest worry. Namely, it is the way in which Cleopatra has been presented to future generations. Cleopatra herself expressed her worry in the following comment:

> "saucy lictors
> Will catch at us, like strumpets; and scald rhymers
> Ballad us out o' tune: the quick comedians
> Extemporally will stage us, and present
> Our Alexandrian revels; Antony
> Shall be brought drunken forth, and I shall see
> Some squeaking Cleopatra boy my greatness
> I' the posture of a whore."

Shakespeare immortalized Cleopatra's worry by making her one of the most attractive heroines of his plays. For centuries she has been represented by "some squeaking Cleopatra boy" actors that have been parading through the stages of various theatres all over the world. In this way Cleopatra's secret has been exposed to generations of spectators who have been warned about her charm, her approaches, and her wicked aim.

2.4 Return to the Vicious Circle in "Titus Andronicus"

Introduction

"Titus Andronicus" portrays events derived from the history of the late Roman Empire, but which are entirely fictitious. The play depicts a fictional Roman general engaged in a cycle of revenge with his enemy Tamora, the Queen of the Goths.

The Goths were East Germanic tribes who, in the 3rd and 4th centuries, harassed the Roman Empire. In the 5th and 6th centuries, they were divided as the Visigoths and the Ostrogoths. It was a Visigothic force led by Alaric I that sacked Rome in 410. The Visigoths and the Ostrogoths established powerful successor-states of the Roman Empire in the Iberian Peninsula and Italy, respectively.

This play is by far Shakespeare's bloodiest work. It lost its popularity during the Victorian era because of its gore, and has only recently begun to revive its fortunes. It has even been suggested by a group of scholars that, due to the "un-Shakespearean barbarity" of the play, Shakespeare did not write it at all. By now the readers may realize that Shakespeare's plays are a unique example of "illustrative history" in English literature, i.e., they are designed to depict a series of events that reflect the evolutionary process. Therefore, their meaning cannot be unfolded by using conventional scholarly techniques and methodologies. Ordinary social, emotional or intellectual criteria do not apply to the interpretation of the evolutionary process.

"Titus Andronicus" describes the last stage of the Roman evolutionary cycle.

Technical background

Initially humanity was in such a condition, that the self faculty was totally engrossed in organizing basic survival and selfish actions. At that time, therefore, spiritual teaching was limited to the outward form of laws that aimed at controlling the self faculty. It was for this reason that ancient mystics used to place the most emphasis on the reforming of the self faculty and regarded the purification merely as the end product and eventual consummation of such training. After some time had passed there appeared certain people who immersed themselves in an indiscriminate application of the outward laws. These people started to show signs of extreme rigidity in their meticulous obedience to customs and rituals. Thus, without taking into account the question of proportion, and without making a proper diagnosis, they proposed one single medicine for every ailment. They maintained that man's only obstacle was his own self, his habits and behaviour.

In "Titus Andronicus" Shakespeare describes an example of such an indiscriminate application of laws.

Storyline

Titus Andronicus, a Roman general, returns from ten years' campaigning against the Goths. He has captured Tamora, Queen of the Goths, her three sons, and Aaron, her lover. In obedience to Roman rituals, Titus sacrifices Tamora's eldest son, which earns him Tamora's unending hatred and her promise of revenge.

The Tribune of the People, Marcus Andronicus, announces that Titus Andronicus, who is Marcus' brother, has been chosen by the people to be their new emperor. However, Titus Andronicus refuses the throne in favour of the late emperor's eldest son Saturninus. Titus and Saturninus agree that Saturninus will marry Titus' daughter Lavinia. However, Bassianus, a younger brother of Saturninus, had been previously betrothed to the girl. Bassianus and Lavinia, with the help of Titus' sons, escape the marriage. Titus is angry with his sons for bringing what he sees as dishonour upon his name. In a fight he kills his own son Mutius.

Publicly humiliated by the loss of Lavinia, Saturninus announces that he will instead take Tamora as empress. Aaron schemes with

Tamora to murder Bassianus and have Titus' two sons, Martius and Quintus, framed for the murder. At the same time Aaron urges Tamora's sons, Chiron and Demetrius, to rape Lavinia. After the rape they cut off her hands and tongue so she cannot give their crime away. Titus and his eldest son Lucius beg Saturninus for the lives of Martius and Quintus. However, Martius and Quintus are found guilty and are marched off to execution. At this moment Aaron arrives and falsely tells Titus, Lucius, and Marcus that the emperor will spare the lives of Titus' sons if one of them sacrifices a hand. Each demands the right to do so, but it is Titus whose hand is hacked off by Aaron. In return, a messenger arrives from Saturninus and brings the heads of Titus' two sons. Lucius is banished from Rome. He raises an army among the Goths.

Each of these misfortunes hits the aged and tired Titus with heavier and heavier impact. Eventually, he begins to act oddly and everyone assumes that he has become mad. In his madness Titus ties written prayers for justice to arrows and commands his kinsmen to send them into the sky. However, Marcus redirects the arrows to land inside the palace of Saturninus. This enrages Saturninus. He orders the execution of the Clown who had delivered a further supplication from Titus.

Tamora delivers a mixed-race child and a nurse says that Aaron must have fathered it. Aaron kills the nurse and flees with the baby to save it from the Emperor's inevitable wrath. Lucius, marching on Rome with an army, captures Aaron and sentences him to be hanged. Aaron makes a deal with Lucius. To save the baby Aaron reveals the entire plot, relishing every murder, rape and dismemberment.

Tamora, convinced of Titus' madness, approaches him along with her two sons, dressed as spirits of Revenge, Murder, and Rape. She tells Titus that she, as a supernatural spirit, will grant him revenge if he convinces Lucius to stop his attack on Rome. Titus agrees and then tricks her. He captures her sons, kills them, and makes a pie out of them. He feeds this pie to their mother. Afterwards Titus kills Tamora and Lavinia. Saturninus kills Titus just as Lucius arrives. Lucius kills Saturninus to avenge his father's death.

Lucius tells his family's story to the people and is proclaimed Emperor. He orders that Saturninus be given a proper burial, that Tamora's body be thrown to the wild beasts, and that Aaron be buried chest-deep and left to die of thirst and starvation.

Rome: 4th century AD

The play describes the evolutionary state of Rome at the end of the Roman cycle. By looking at the changes that Rome went through between the times of "Coriolanus" and "Titus Andronicus" may help to understand Shakespeare's presentation of the Roman cycle. In this way the readers may see what progress, if any, has been achieved as the result of its exposure to unitive energy.

Lavinia represents an element of creative energy that has been embedded within the Roman cycle. Rome has been exposed to, or coated with, creative energy several times. Specifically, this particular element was "coloured" or designated for the Roman heart. This element of creative energy was previously represented by Virgilia in "Coriolanus", Calphurnia in "Julius Caesar", and Fulvia in "Antony and Cleopatra". Yet, this element has not been fully assimilated yet. Its utilization has been restrained by the presence of corrupted aspects. Shakespeare indicates that this element of creative energy has not had a chance to fulfill its developmental potential within the Roman cycle. At the end of "Titus Andronicus" this element is deactivated. This is symbolically illustrated as Lavinia's brutal rape followed by her death.

It is obvious that 4th century Rome is still in a pretty much degenerated state. The leading aspects of this being are either ignorant, corrupted or are under the influence of destructive elements. The modus operandi of Rome is currently driven by revenge.

It looks that the tribunes have not been changed either. Here is Titus' comment about the Roman tribunes:

> "Rome could afford no tribune like to these.
> A stone is soft as wax -tribunes more hard than stones;

A stone is silent, and offendeth not,
And tribunes with their tongues doom men to death."

The sophistry of the destructive agents corresponds to the spiritual state of the being. The more degenerate a being the more simplistic and cruel are the forces that are attached to it. At the time of "Coriolanus" it was Brutus, then it was Cassius in "Julius Caesar" and Cleopatra in "Antony and Cleopatra" that played the role of the whisperers. Now it is Aaron, Tamora's lover, who represents the destructive agent that is attached to Rome. There is no comparison between the degree of cruelty that is exercised by Aaron and the behaviour of his predecessors. Shakespeare emphasizes this point by purposely making the play his bloodiest work: "Titus Andronicus" is a play with 14 killings, 6 severed members, 1 rape, 1 live burial and 1 case of cannibalism.

Aaron - the villain

The character of Aaron is the portrait of a wicked aspect that is able to explore fully and mercilessly all weaknesses of Rome. It should be pointed out that Aaron's means are rather simple ones. Aaron merely explores the Romans' naivety, ignorance, and their rudimentary attachments to customs and beliefs. At the same time he is able to use for his purpose the Goths' craving for lust and revenge.

Again and again, Aaron is able to execute his atrocious plans. The audience may be under the impression that Aaron can go unchecked with exercising his destructive plots. Like most of Shakespeare's villains, Aaron does not hide from the audience his evil aims:

> "… kill a man, or else devise his death,
> Ravish a maid, or plot the way to do it,
> Accuse some innocent and forswear myself,
> Set deadly enmity between two friends,
> Make poor men's cattle break their necks;
> Set fire on barns and hay-stacks in the night,
> And bid the owners quench them with their tears.

Oft have I digg'd up dead men from their graves,
And set them upright at their dear friends' doors."

Even at the end, when he is left to die, Aaron is unrepentant and proclaims that:

"If one good Deed in all my life I did,
I do repent it from my very Soule."

Aaron uses Tamora as a partner in his vicious plots. Tamora is a symbol of barbarism, savagery, and unrestrained lasciviousness. Tamora's sons, Chiron and Demetrius, enhance even further these elements of cruelty and brutality. Shakespeare emphasizes the fact that Tamora and her sons are the fruit of the seed of cruelty that was cultivated in Rome at the time of "Coriolanus". The "gilded wings fly" episode provides a link. In this episode Titus reprimands Marcus for killing a fly:

"But how, if that fly had a father and mother?
How would he hang his slender gilded wings,
And buzz lamenting doings in the air! "

Marcus explains that the fly represents Aaron, the empress' Moor:

"Pardon me, sir; it was a black ill-favor'd fly,
Like to the empress' Moor; therefore I kill'd him."

The audience may recognize that the most cruel scenes in "Titus Andronicus" are derivatives of the episode from "Coriolanus" when the young Martius caught a "gilded butterfly", tore it to pieces with his teeth and "he mammocked it". The butterfly episode is replayed in the scene where Titus urges his brother and Lavinia to help him carry off stage the severed heads of two of his sons and his own severed hand:

"Come, brother, take a head;
And in this hand the other I will bear.
Lavinia, thou shalt be employ'd: these arms!
Bear thou my hand, sweet wench, between thy
teeth."

Later on Titus makes pie out of Tamora's sons and feeds the pie to their mother so she *mammocks* it.

It should be noted though, that Aaron managed to commit his greatest mischief just before he is buried chest-deep and left to die of thirst and starvation. When a Goth soldier brings the fugitive Aaron along with his baby, Lucius' initial impulse is to hang the father and the child, letting the child hang first so that the father will have to watch. The Goths bring a ladder and make Aaron climb it. However, Aaron, while on the gibbet, makes a bargain with Lucius to preserve the child in exchange for disclosing all the horrors that he has committed. In this way Aaron is able to preserve his roots in Rome. By preserving the life of his baby Aaron re-implanted in Rome a seed of destructivity. As the readers will see, this seed will grow to its malignant form at the inception of the most recent evolutionary cycle (see Volume 4, Chapter 8).

Ruthless forest

Banishment in Shakespeare's plays marks the inception of the reformation process. In "Titus Andronicus" it is Lucius who is banished from Rome. Lucius goes to look for support among the Goths. Here is Titus' comment to Lucius:

> " ... how happy art thou, then,
> From these devourers to be banished!"

Banishment may lead through a heath or a forest. A forest symbolically indicates a lower (earthly) inspirational state, which provides an environment allowing for uplifting of selected aspects and elimination of incongruent ones. There is such a forest near Rome in "Titus Andronicus". This forest was not existent at the time of "Coriolanus". For a brief period an intermediary inspirational state was activated during the wine drinking party at the time of Octavius Caesar. Now, however, the forest is described as "ruthless, dreadful, deaf, and dull". Here is Aaron's comment to Chiron and Demetrius:

"The woods are ruthless, dreadful, deaf, and dull;
There speak, and strike, brave boys, and take your turns;
There serve your lusts, shadow'd from heaven's eye,
And revel in Lavinia's treasury."

Therefore, this forest would have to be cleared first, before it could regain its developmental function. In its current state, this wild forest is used by Aaron to scheme the murder of Bassianus, the rape of Lavinia, and set-up a trap for Titus' two sons, Martius and Quintus.

Protective agency

Marcus, the brother of Titus, is the only aspect that is neither corrupted nor affected by the presence of destructive elements. Whereas everyone else has had a hand in at least one murder or crime, he remains noticeably removed from the bloodshed. Marcus' role in the process is limited to being an observer and a commentator. On one occasion, however, Marcus actively intervenes in the process. This is possible because Marcus, unlike Menenius in "Coriolanus", is linked to the transmission chain. This link was reinstated by Octavius Caesar at the time of "Antony and Cleopatra". Marcus' intervention proves to be critical to Rome.

By now the readers may realize that it was Titus' actions that triggered a chain of destructive events in Rome. Titus follows Roman customs and beliefs in a rather rudimentary and mechanical manner. He shows extreme rigidity in his meticulous and senseless obedience to Roman rituals. Therefore, any change in the course of events could only be induced by a substantial adjustment in Titus' behaviour. At one point Titus asks for help from heavens. He ties written prayers for justice to arrows and commands his kinsmen to aim them at the heavenly gods:

"… Then, when you come to Pluto's region,
I pray you, deliver him this petition;
Tell him, it is for justice and for aid,
And that it comes from old Andronicus,
Shaken with sorrows in ungrateful Rome."

...

"We will solicit heaven and move the gods
To send down Justice for to wreak our wrongs."

At this very moment Titus goes beyond his usual mechanical obedience to Roman rituals. He sincerely asks for help from above. Therefore, help is granted to him. For a brief time an invisible protective agency is activated. Up to this moment this protective agency was inactive. When Titus sincerely asks for help, Marcus is able to activate it. Marcus tells his kinsmen to redirect the arrows and send them instead into Saturninus' court:

"Kinsmen, shoot all your shafts into the court:
We will afflict the emperor in his pride."

And then Marcus tells Titus:

"My lord, I aim a mile beyond the moon;
Your letter is with Jupiter by this."

Marcus' intervention is a very subtle one. However, it is incredibly effective. Marcus' apparently insignificant gesture changes the entire course of events. From this point on, the destructive forces are on the diminishing end.

The significance of the moment is marked by the appearance of the Clown. As indicated earlier, the appearance of the Clown points out the critical moment of the process. Titus, in his apparent insanity, treats the Clown as a messenger from heaven:

"News, news from heaven! Marcus, the post is come.
Sirrah, what tidings? have you any letters?
Shall I have justice? what says Jupiter?"

There is a double play in the above scene. The Clown's appearance seemingly helps to display Titus' insanity when he mistakes him for a messenger from Jupiter. The Clown, however, delivers a very precise message:

> "O, the gibbet-maker! he says that he hath taken
> them down again, for the man must not be hanged till
> the next week."

The Clown says that Titus' role is limited to that of a "gibbet-maker", i.e., an executioner of destructive elements. He also says that the requested justice has to be postponed "till the next week".

Marcus' action marks the beginning of the end for the destructive aspects. Immediately afterwards the negative forces become agitated, disturbed and weakened. Saturninus becomes furious about the arrows flying "about the streets of Rome", for they have advertised his crimes to all:

> "And now he writes to heaven for his redress:
> See, here's to Jove, and this to Mercury;
> This to Apollo; this to the god of war;
> Sweet scrolls to fly about the streets of Rome!"

Saturninus flies into a panic when he hears that Lucius has gathered an army of Goths and is already advancing on Rome. He had already heard rumours that the people would support Lucius over him. At this point Shakespeare makes a direct reference to "Coriolanus" to emphasize the link between the first and last stages of the Roman cycle. Here is Æmilius' comment to Saturninus:

> "Arm, arm, my lord; Rome never had more cause.
> The Goths have gather'd head; and with a power
> high-resolved men, bent to the spoil,
> They hither march amain, under conduct
> Of Lucius, son to old Andronicus;
> Who threats, in course of this revenge, to do
> As much as ever Coriolanus did."

At the same time Tamora loses the support of Aaron. When she requests that Aaron kill their baby, he decides to escape to the Goths. Now Tamora is acting alone. This explains why suddenly her scheming becomes simplistic, naïve, and ineffective. Tamora promises Saturninus that she, similarly to Volumnia in "Coriolanus", can persuade Titus to entreat Lucius to give up his war efforts. Tamora approaches Titus disguised as a spirit of Revenge along with her two sons dressed as the spirits of Murder and Rape. This naïve and simplistic costume-show is supposed to convince Titus that he should stop Lucius from invading Rome. Now, however, the roles have changed. Titus is able to trick Tamora and kill her sons. In the final scenes Titus kills his daughter Lavinia and stabs Tamora; Saturninus kills Titus; Lucius kills Saturninus.

The protective agency, such as that activated in "Titus Andronicus", may protect a being against its spiritual extinction. Such mechanisms, however, are not capable of bringing a being onto a higher stage of development. At the end of "Titus Andronicus" the impulse of creative energy is deactivated and removed. Without an active element of creative energy there is no chance for the formation of an evolutionary triad. Rome becomes spiritually sterile.

The time period that followed the events described in "Titus Andronicus" is known in the history of Europe as the Dark Ages. This was a period of disorder among events, confusion among men, processes without design, humanity without direction.

Limitation of outward forms of laws

It is interesting to see how Shakespeare emphasizes the limitation of developmental approaches that are based on outward forms of laws. Shakespeare shows this by drawing a parallel between an indiscriminate application of the laws and the reliance on outdated developmental methodologies encoded in ancient myths. Shakespeare often uses various references to episodes from Greek and Roman myths to emphasize this point.

In this context it should be recalled that the plot of "Titus Andronicus" includes an episode of Ovid's Procne and Philomela. Shakespeare gives direct references to Ovid's "Metamorphoses" in which the story is included. Firstly, it is Aaron who makes a reference to it while talking to Tamora:

> "This is the day of doom for Bassianus:
> His Philomel must lose her tongue to-day,
> Thy sons make pillage of her chastity
> And wash their hands in Bassianus' blood."

Then, it is Lavinia who wants to get Titus' and Marcus' attention to "Metamorphoses" which Young Lucius is carrying. When Titus asks Young Lucius:

> "Lucius, what book is that she tosseth so?"

he answers:

> "Grandsire, 'tis Ovid's Metamorphoses;
> My mother gave it me."

When Lavinia gets to the book she turns through its pages until she reaches the story of Philomela. In this story Tereus raped his sister-in-law Philomela and then cut off her tongue so that she couldn't reveal the crime. Philomela then wove a tapestry that told her story and had it sent to her sister Procne, who was Tereus' wife. In revenge, Procne killed their son and served him to Tereus, who unknowingly ate him.

In "Titus Andronicus" Chiron and Demetrius raped Lavinia. After the rape Chiron and Demetrius, apparently learning from Philomena's story, cut off Lavinia's tongue and her hands, so she could neither tell nor weave away their crime. However, Marcus is able to extract from Lavinia her story by asking her to write in the sand the name of the culprits. Holding the staff with her mouth and guiding it with her stumps, Lavinia writes that Chiron and Demetrius raped her (*stuprum* means "rape" in Latin):

> "Stuprum. Chiron. Demetrius."

After a brief moment of sincerity, Titus returns to his old routines. This is illustrated by Titus' execution of Tamora's sons. Titus' revenge is an "overreached" copy of Procne's story:

"I know them all, though they suppose me mad,
And will o'erreach them in their own devices."

...

"For worse than Philomel you used my daughter,
And worse than Procne I will be revenged."

Titus, after killing Chiron and Demetrius, grinds their bones to dust and makes a paste of it with their blood, which he turns into "coffins", a word that also meant "pie crust". He then bakes Tamora's sons in their "coffins" and serves the dish to their mother at a banquet.

At the end of the play Titus further reconfirms his role as a blind executioner, the role that was foretold by the Clown. Titus asks Saturninus if Virginius, a heroic Centurion from a Greek story, should have slain Virginia, his daughter, because she had been raped. When Saturninus responds that a girl should not survive her shame, Titus kills Lavinia.

In summary, Shakespeare emphasizes the limited use of ancient myths in the developmental process. He also made a direct reference to this particular episode in "As You Like It". Touchstone, the Fool, makes the following comment to Audrey, a goatherd:

"I am here with thee and thy goats, as the most
capricious poet, honest Ovid, was among the Goths."

The readers may realize that, in "Titus Andronicus", the ancient myth was used merely as a template for wicked scheming and intensified cruelty.

Conclusion

"Titus Andronicus" concludes the Roman Plays. By describing the Roman cycle in four plays, Shakespeare points out that the cycle did not come to its completion. The Roman cycle was terminated at the stage corresponding to "Richard III" in the History Plays. This means that Rome was not able to develop enough inner strength to bring itself onto the next evolutionary stage.

The main reason of the failure was Rome's incapacity to integrate creative energy. Shakespeare traces this incapacity back to the time of the foundation of Rome. In other words, the foundation of Rome was not correctly implemented. The circumstances that led to such an inopportune inception of Rome are explained in "The Tempest" (see Volume 4, Chapter 8).

Shakespeare indicates that a long time before Rome's failure a rescue was already foreseen and initiated in another place on the planet. The rescue of this particular geographical area was part of a complex operation implemented in Western Europe. The details of this operation are described in "Pericles, Prince of Tire" (see Volume 2, Chapter 4).

CHAPTER 3

Celtic Evolutionary Cycle

3.1 Partial Reformation in "King Lear"

Introduction

Shakespeare's History Plays describe the process induced by a contact with evolutionary energy. A question may be asked, what happens if a person, a country, or an entire culture has not been able, for whatever reason, to sustain its previously injected evolutionary impulse?

Shakespeare described such a situation in the Roman tetralogy. A similar situation is illustrated in the Celtic trilogy. The Celtic trilogy includes "King Lear", "Cymbeline", and "Macbeth".

"King Lear" is based on various accounts of the semi-legendary King Leir, a king of pre-Roman Britain, whose tale was first written down by the 12th century historian Geoffrey of Monmouth, one of the major figures in the development of British history and the popularity of King Arthur's tales.

Technical background

Evolutionary gains may be obtained only within an intentionally created environment of friction. Such an approach may appear to be strange and contrary to ordinary human judgment. However, such an approach is allowed by the measure of freewill that man has and its consequences may not be annulled by evolutionary forces, no matter how much is at stake. All that may be done is to arrange situations that will provide additional opportunities for man to choose differently. Consequently, as long as the evolutionary process advances accordingly to its potential, such activity will be supported. However, as soon as the activity begins to diverge from its developmental possibilities, evolutionary energies will be separated from it. At a certain stage of divergence, i.e., when nothing more can be salvaged, the evolutionary impulse(s) will be withdrawn entirely. At this point the process becomes subject to the law of diminishing returns and finally

127

extinguishes itself.

However, there are natural mechanisms that may protect a being against its total extinction. Namely, there are several forms of protective layers that may prevent a person, a group of people, a country, or an entire culture against evolutionary extinction. In the case of a person, a protective layer may take the form of an aspect of his inner being. In the case of a country or a culture, such a layer may be invested into a person or a group of people.

There is an equivalent mechanism that has been identified in the way physical organs function. For example, when heart arteries are clogged and this blocks the blood flow, there is a natural mechanism that may kick-in secondary arteries that may prolong the functioning of the body. It means that the human body has self-protecting mechanisms to preserve its life. Similarly, the human inner being may be preserved by inner protective layers. In Shakespeare's plays, such a protective layer is represented by a household, a city, or a country. For example, the city of Antium represents such a protective layer in "Coriolanus". In "King Lear" another form of secondary layer is presented.

Storyline

King Lear, an aging king of Britain, decides to step down from the throne and to divide his kingdom among his three daughters. First, however, he puts his daughters through a test, asking each to tell him how much she loves him. Goneril and Regan, Lear's elder daughters, give their father flattering answers. But Cordelia, Lear's youngest and favourite daughter, tells him that she has no words to describe how much she loves her father. King Lear flies into a rage and disowns Cordelia. The king of France, who has courted Cordelia, decides to take Cordelia even without her dowry. They both leave to France.

Soon afterwards, King Lear realizes that he made a wrong decision. Goneril and Regan swiftly begin to undermine the little authority that Lear still holds. King Lear flees his daughters' houses to wander on a heath during a thunderstorm, accompanied by his

Fool and by Kent, a loyal nobleman in disguise.

Meanwhile, the Duke of Gloucester also experiences similar family problems. His illegitimate son, Edmund, tricks him into believing that Gloucester's legitimate son, Edgar, is trying to kill him. Edgar flees the manhunt that his father has set for him by disguising himself as a crazy beggar. Like Lear, he heads out onto the heath.

When Gloucester realizes that Goneril and Regan have turned against their father, he tries to help Lear. Regan and her husband, the Duke of Cornwall, discover him helping Lear, accuse him of treason, blind him, and turn him out to wander the countryside. Gloucester ends up being led by his disguised son, Edgar, towards the city of Dover, where Lear has also been brought.

In Dover, a French army lands as part of an invasion led by Cordelia in an effort to save her father. Edmund becomes romantically involved with both Goneril and Regan. The Duke of Albany, Goneril's husband, becomes increasingly supportive of Lear. Goneril and Edmund conspire to kill Albany.

The Britain's troops led by Edmund reach Dover. Edmund defeats the Cordelia-led French army. Lear and Cordelia are captured. In the climactic scene, Edgar duels with and kills Edmund. The readers learn of the death of Gloucester. Goneril poisons Regan out of jealousy over Edmund and then kills herself when her treachery is revealed to her husband. By Edmund's order, Cordelia is executed in prison. Lear dies out of grief at Cordelia's death.

Albany, Edgar, and the elderly Kent are left to take care of the kingdom.

Britain: 10th century BC

As each of Shakespeare's plays, "King Lear" illustrates a being at a certain stage of the evolutionary cycle. The main characters of the play represent various aspects of the being of Britain. The leading aspects are King Lear, his elder daughters Goneril and Regan, their husbands Albany and Cornwall, the noblemen Kent and

Gloucester, and Goneril's servant Oswald.

Shakespeare portraits a woman as a symbol of an impulse of evolutionary energy. The assimilation of an evolutionary impulse is symbolically described as a marriage. Cordelia, King Lear's youngest daughter, represents such an impulse of evolutionary energy. This impulse is ready to induce a higher functioning of Britain. In order to fully discharge her potentiality, Cordelia would need the assistance of King Lear. Only in this way would it be possible to form an evolutionary triad.

King Lear symbolizes the leading aspect of the intellect faculty. This aspect, for whatever reason, has not been developed according to its needs and potential. As has been mentioned in the background, such a situation is allowed by the measure of freewill that the being has and its consequences may not be annulled, no matter how much is at stake. All that may be done is to contrive such situations that will provide increased opportunities for the being to choose differently. The entire play is about such contrived situations that may bring Britain back onto the right path.

King Lear is used to enjoying absolute power and flattery, and he does not respond well to being contradicted or challenged. He wishes to maintain the power of a king while unburdening himself of the responsibility. This is illustrated in the scene where King Lear announces his plans concerning the kingdom:

> "Know that we have divided
> In three our kingdom: and 'tis our fast intent
> To shake all cares and business from our age;
> Conferring them on younger strengths, while we
> Unburthen'd crawl toward death."

Cordelia is his favourite daughter. Therefore, King Lear intends to give his largest gift to her:

> "... what can you say to draw
> A third more opulent than your sisters?"

King Lear expects that Cordelia will comply with his wishes. He wants Cordelia to demonstrate openly and publicly her obedience to him. However, Cordelia's functionality is too advanced to be bent down to that of her father's wishes. Cordelia remains silent:

> "What shall Cordelia do?
> Love, and be silent."
>   …
> "I am sure, my love's
> More richer than my tongue."

When King Lear insists, then Cordelia tries to explain to him:

> "Good my lord,
> You have begot me, bred me, loved me: I
> Return those duties back as are right fit,
> Obey you, love you, and most honour you.
> Why have my sisters husbands, if they say
> They love you all? Haply, when I shall wed,
> That lord whose hand must take my plight shall carry
> Half my love with him, half my care and duty:
> Sure, I shall never marry like my sisters,
> To love my father all."

King Lear does not understand the meaning of Cordelia's words. In her answer to King Lear she points out the limitations of ordinary love. King Lear does not comprehend the situation and its potential. He is incapable of realizing what the role of Cordelia is. Instead, he flies into a rage and disowns her.

The king of France knows what the true role of Cordelia is. His function is to protect Cordelia. It is important to observe that there is no man from Britain among those who court Cordelia. At this time, therefore, there is no possibility to form an evolutionary triad within Britain. When the duke of Burgundy rejects her, the king of France takes Cordelia with him to France. At this moment Britain loses its finest component. Britain becomes developmentally sterile.

It should be pointed out that the action of "King Lear" takes place in the 10th century BC (est.). At that time France did not exist yet as a kingdom; the Frankish kingdom was established in the 5th century AD. France, therefore, is an entity that exists in the future. This symbolically indicates that "France" represents a higher state that operates outside the limitations of conventional time. It is important to notice that the relationship between the king of France and Cordelia is based on the code of chivalry and courtly love. In other words, the king of France is a Knight of Chivalry. This is reflected by his manner of addressing Cordelia. The king does not refer to Cordelia as his wife but as "queen of us, of ours, and our fair France":

> "Fairest Cordelia, that art most rich, being poor;
> Most choice, forsaken; and most loved, despised!
> Thee and thy virtues here I seize upon:
> Be it lawful I take up what's cast away.
> Gods, gods! 'tis strange that from their cold'st neglect
> My love should kindle to inflamed respect.
> Thy dowerless daughter, king, thrown to my chance,
> Is queen of us, of ours, and our fair France:
> Not all the dukes of waterish Burgundy
> Can buy this unprized precious maid of me.
> Bid them farewell, Cordelia, though unkind:
> Thou losest here, a better where to find."

Cordelia's departure to France marks the withdrawal of this particular evolutionary impulse from Britain.

The Earl of Kent is a loyal supporter of King Lear. Here is how Kent describes his relationship with King Lear:

> "Royal Lear,
> Whom I have ever honour'd as my king,
> Loved as my father, as my master follow'd,
> As my great patron thought on in my prayers."

Kent realizes that King Lear has made a fundamental mistake. Kent is impulsive and blunt. And he cannot control his feelings and reactions:

> "When Lear is mad. What wilt thou do, old man?

Think'st thou that duty shall have dread to speak,
When power to flattery bows? To plainness honour's
bound,
When majesty stoops to folly. Reverse thy doom."

...

"My life I never held but as a pawn
To wage against thy enemies; nor fear to lose it,
Thy safety being the motive."

Kent has to pay a price for his behaviour. King Lear punishes him by banishing him from the kingdom:

"Five days we do allot thee, for provision
To shield thee from diseases of the world;
And on the sixth to turn thy hated back
Upon our kingdom: if, on the tenth day following,
Thy banish'd trunk be found in our dominions,
The moment is thy death. Away! by Jupiter,
This shall not be revoked."

Kent disguises himself as a peasant and calls himself Caius. Under this disguise he returns to the court and is employed by King Lear as his servant.

These actions of King Lear trigger destructive activities which are immediately initiated by King Lear's elder daughters. Goneril challenges Lear's authority, and later on boldly wrests military power away from her husband. Regan, King Lear's middle daughter, is as ruthless as Goneril and as aggressive in all the same ways.

Some aspects of Britain are under the influence of Goneril and Regan. Their husbands, the Duke of Albany and the Duke of Cornwall, represent these aspects. Cornwall, the husband of Regan, is domineering, cruel, violent, and he works together with his wife and sister-in-law. Albany, the husband of Goneril, realizes the evil and cruelty of Goneril, Regan, and Cornwall. However, he is indecisive and lacks foresight. It is only later on in the play that he changes his attitude and becomes an active supporter of King Lear.

Goneril's servant, Oswald, represents a corrupted aspect of the self faculty. Here is how Oswald is described by Kent:

> "A knave; a rascal; an eater of broken meats; a
> base, proud, shallow, beggarly, three-suited,
> hundred-pound, filthy, worsted-stocking knave; a
> lily-livered, action-taking knave, a whoreson,
> glass-gazing, super-serviceable finical rogue;
> one-trunk-inheriting slave; one that wouldst be a
> bawd, in way of good service, and art nothing but
> the composition of a knave, beggar, coward, pandar,
> and the son and heir of a mongrel bitch."

The result of King Lear's decision is that the entire process which had been put in place earlier is derailed. King Lear cuts himself off from constructive participation in the process. The primary layer of Britain is deactivated. This situation may be compared to clogging the main heart artery or to burning off the fuses of a main electrical circuit.

In order to secure some remaining residual developmental potential, a corrective action is necessary. In this particular case, the corrective action is implemented by activating the secondary layer of Britain. Any residual development that is still possible to achieve may be realized by switching on the secondary layer.

The secondary layer

The secondary layer of Britain is represented by Gloucester's household. It consists of the Earl of Gloucester, his two sons, Edgar and Edmund, and servants.

Gloucester's household is part of the kingdom of Britain. Gloucester is a chieftain who rules over a territory on behalf of King Lear. In other words, Gloucester's household represents a secondary layer of Britain's heart faculty. It may be compared to the above-mentioned secondary blood arteries that may be activated when the main arteries have been clogged.

Gloucester's household has a similar structure to that of King Lear's court. It is like its mirror reflection. The audience can see that the dynamics of the relationship within King Lear's court is projected onto Gloucester's household. Gloucester is honest and loyal. However, he is a bit gullible. Similarly to King Lear, he acts naively and makes his decisions hastily.

The most important feature of the secondary layer is the presence of Edgar. Edgar is Gloucester's elder and legitimate son. Edgar is the most developed aspect of Britain. Edgar is King Lear's godson. This is indicated by Regan in her comment to Gloucester:

> "What, did my father's godson seek your life?
> He whom my father named? your Edgar?"

In this way Shakespeare indicates that there is a spiritual link between these two layers. This link forms the crucial ingredient of the entire inner structure of Britain. Through this link, Britain is provided with the leading constructive aspect. (The readers will notice that this link carries a much higher degree of expediency than that between Rome and Antium in "Coriolanus"). It may be presumed that Cordelia was designated for this aspect of Britain's heart which is represented by Edgar. However, King Lear's badly timed decisions have thwarted the process.

Edgar is loyal and trusting but he is still immature and naïve. He is not yet ready for this role. First, he has to go through a number of preparatory experiences. By dressing himself as a beggar he manages to escape the trap that is set-up by Edmund, his half-brother:

> "Whiles I may 'scape,
> I will preserve myself: and am bethought
> To take the basest and most poorest shape
> That ever penury, in contempt of man,
> Brought near to beast: my face I'll grime with filth;
> Blanket my loins: elf all my hair in knots;
> And with presented nakedness out-face
> The winds and persecutions of the sky."

Edgar's faith and trust in his father allows him to avoid the trap.

The villain

Edmund, the bastard son of Gloucester, was away for nine years and has just arrived. It seems that these previous nine years were quite constructive for Britain. Similarly to the appearance of Richard III in the History Plays, Edmund's arrival on the scene marks the transition to the next stage of the process.

Edmund's desire to use any means possible to secure his own desires makes him a villain. He follows a simple rule:

> "Let me, if not by birth, have lands by wit:
> All with me's meet that I can fashion fit."

In the course of the events, Edmund, the bastard, gradually becomes the leading force for all the destructive tendencies.

The Fool

The Fool in "King Lear" represents a guiding aspect. A fool, or a madman, is often used in teaching stories to describe a guide. This is nicely summarized by the following comments by another Shakespeare's fool, Touchstone, in "As You Like It": "The fool doth think he is wise, but the wise man knows himself to be a fool".

The Fool is a constant companion to King Lear. The Fool uses double-talk to criticize King Lear for his actions and mistakes. We may assume that for the last nine years he was tutoring Cordelia. He has been her spiritual guardian. He was preparing her for her role in the development of Britain. However, King Lear's recent foolish decisions have frustrated the entire process. The Fool indicates this to King Lear:

> "Thou shouldst not have been old till thou hadst
> been wise."

...

> "When thou clovest thy crown i' the middle, and
> gavest away both parts, thou borest thy ass on thy
> back o'er the dirt"

The Fool seems to be strongly affected by Cordelia's departure:

> "Since my young lady's going into France, sir, the
> fool hath much pined away."

Nevertheless, the Fool has to continue his work. As long as there is a chance that Britain may fulfill even a fraction of its evolutionary potential, such an activity has to be supported. Despite the foolishness of Lear, the Fool's presence is still critical. This is why the Fool decides to leave the court and accompany Lear in his wandering through the country side:

> "She that's a maid now, and laughs at my departure,
> Shall not be a maid long, unless things be cut shorter."

The Fool has to implement a provisional plan of action, otherwise "things (would) be cut shorter". The provisional plan requires the activation of Britain's secondary layer.

The process

There is a time limit for each phase of the evolutionary process. At the beginning of the play we are witnessing the end of such a phase. The aspect of the intellect faculty, which is represented by King Lear, has been stabilized below its potential. King Lear was supposed to be the leading aspect of Britain's evolutionary triad. In other words, in the allotted time the leading aspect of Britain has not achieved its desired and needed progress. Therefore, it is necessary to implement a corrective action.

As discussed in the History Plays and illustrated in "Julius Caesar", there are some basic rules that govern the process. One of these rules requires that the constructive aspects need to be preserved. Another rule indicates that all corrupted aspects have to be eliminated. Yet another rule states that these aspects that have not fulfilled their evolutionary potential should be partially purified before they are discharged. The plot of "King Lear" consistently follows these rules.

In this phase of the process the Fool has to change his approach. For example, the Fool delegates some tasks to Kent. This is illustrated in the scene when he gives his jester's cap to Kent. This happens when Kent, disguised as a peasant, starts to serve King Lear:

> "Let me hire him too: here's my coxcomb."

And then the Fool gives Kent some instructions:

> "We'll set thee to school to an ant, to teach thee
> there's no labouring i' the winter. All that follow
> their noses are led by their eyes but blind men; and
> there's not a nose among twenty but can smell him
> that's stinking. Let go thy hold when a great wheel
> runs down a hill, lest it break thy neck with
> following it: but the great one that goes up the
> hill, let him draw thee after. When a wise man
> gives thee better counsel, give me mine again."

The Fool clearly indicates to Kent that Lear's role has been downgraded; now there is "the great one" that is going to move the process upwards.

The storm

Some disturbances at the lower level are transmitted to the invisible world. This in turn triggers a chain of far-reaching consequences that impacts the entire environment.

There are signs of such a chain-reaction in "King Lear". The actions of King Lear have been conjugated with the immediate invisible world. As the result, some events on a larger scale have been instigated. Shakespeare describes these events as seen from the perspective of two perceptions, i.e., Gloucester's view and Edmund's explanation. Gloucester's view represents a superstitious perception. Here is how Gloucester sees and understands them:

> "These late eclipses in the sun and moon portend
> no good to us: though the wisdom of nature can
> reason it thus and thus, yet nature finds itself
> scourged by the sequent effects: love cools,
> friendship falls off, brothers divide: in
> cities, mutinies; in countries, discord; in
> palaces, treason; and the bond cracked 'twixt son
> and father. This villain of mine comes under the
> prediction; there's son against father: the king
> falls from bias of nature; there's father against
> child. We have seen the best of our time:
> machinations, hollowness, treachery, and all
> ruinous disorders, follow us disquietly to our
> graves."

And then Edmund gives his rational understanding of these events:

> "This is the excellent foppery of the world, that,
> when we are sick in fortune, -often the surfeit
> of our own behavior, -we make guilty of our
> disasters the sun, the moon, and the stars: as
> if we were villains by necessity; fools by
> heavenly compulsion; knaves, thieves, and
> treachers, by spherical predominance; drunkards,
> liars, and adulterers, by an enforced obedience of
> planetary influence; and all that we are evil in,
> by a divine thrusting on: an admirable evasion
> of whoremaster man, to lay his goatish
> disposition to the charge of a star! My
> father compounded with my mother under the
> dragon's tail; and my nativity was under Ursa
> major; so that it follows, I am rough and
> lecherous. Tut, I should have been that I am,
> had the maidenliest star in the firmament
> twinkled on my bastardizing."

The readers will realize that the origin of the events is beyond the comprehension of such simplistic views.

The Fool's final action is taking place on a heath during a great thunderstorm. The Fool has arranged this event and he directs it. All aspects that are needed for such an operation have been assembled there, i.e., King Lear, Edgar, Kent, and Gloucester. All these characters have been, in a certain way, "banished" from their natural environments. The heath symbolically represents the currently available inspirational state. The storm marks the moment when the primary layer is switched "off" and the secondary layer is switched "on":

> "This cold night will turn us all to fools and
> madmen."

At this moment, King Lear is released from his previous charge. Lear's new role is much simpler and his mandate is greatly lowered. The Fool summarizes the situation with his song:

> "He that has and a little tiny wit-
> With hey, ho, the wind and the rain,-
> Must make content with his fortunes fit,
> For the rain it raineth every day."

The Fool indicates that now Lear's mandate has been downgraded, i.e., "must make content with his fortune's fit". Following that, Lear goes through a reforming rebuke. Here is Kent's comment about it:

> "A sovereign shame so elbows him: his own unkindness,
> That stripp'd her from his benediction, turn'd her
> To foreign casualties, gave her dear rights
> To his dog-hearted daughters, these things sting
> His mind so venomously, that burning shame
> Detains him from Cordelia."

During that stormy night Lear experiences some pre-taste of deeper perception. This is the state he has failed to develop in the previous phase of the process. Now Lear starts to perceive the role that

Edgar is going to play in the near future:

"A king, a king!"

However, Lear's behaviour is still overshadowed by his preoccupation with his own vanity, self-importance, and anger towards Goneril and Regan.

Gloucester, the father of Edgar, is not able to recognize this "occasion":

"What, hath your grace no better company?"

Therefore, he will have to go through a series of additional experiences to recover from his "blindness".

It seems that the attendees of the event taking place in a hut on the heath - have gained either clearer vision or better understanding of their new respective roles. This includes Lear, Kent, and most importantly, Edgar. Edgar, who calls himself Tom O'Bedlam, gains a clearer vision ("mark the high noises") of his mission:

"How light and portable my pain seems now,
When that which makes me bend makes the king bow,
He childed as I father'd! Tom, away!
Mark the high noises; and thyself bewray,
When false opinion, whose wrong thought defiles thee,
In thy just proof, repeals and reconciles thee.
What will hap more to-night, safe 'scape the king!"

Edgar is charged with a new responsibility. It is at this point that the Fool leaves the scene:

"And I'll go to bed at noon."

The Fool's role is completed. The various aspects of Britain have been set on their own respective courses.

Roman connection

It is important to emphasize that both, Britain and Rome, had serious difficulties accommodating the previously released evolutionary impulse. This impulse is symbolically represented by Cordelia in "King Lear" and Lavinia in "Titus Andronicus". Both, Cordelia and Lavinia, are capable of inducing a higher functioning of Britain and Rome, respectively. In order to fully discharge their potentiality they would need the support of their fathers. Only in this way would it be possible to form the evolutionary triad. Lear and Titus, however, expect that their daughters should comply with their own selfish plans. They want their daughters to demonstrate their obedience. Neither Lear nor Titus understands the situation and its potentials. Instead, they fly into a rage when their wishes are ignored. They make fundamental errors that set in motion the tragic events that are the subject of these two plays. This similarity between these two plays allows to identify the evolutionary impulse that is represented by Cordelia. Namely, Cordelia, whose "love's more richer than my tongue", represents an element of creative energy. Similarly to Rome, this particular impulse was designated for the purification of Britain's heart. This means that after its deactivation within Britain at the time of "King Lear", this particular impulse was transferred to Rome. First, it appeared in Rome as the eloquently silent Virgilia in "Coriolanus", then as Calphurnia in "Julius Caesar", followed by Fulvia in "Antony and Cleopatra", and finally as tongue-less Lavinia in "Titus Andronicus".

Concluding remarks

At the end of the play the reformation process has been accomplished. The process has followed the previously described rules.

All the corrupted aspects of the being have been eliminated, i.e., Goneril, Regan, Cornwall, Edmund, and Oswald.

Cordelia's attempt to protect Britain with the help of the French army has failed. Cordelia is executed in prison by Edmund's order.

Her death marks the deactivation of this particular evolutionary impulse. Afterwards this particular impulse is transferred to 5th century BC Rome. The appearance of the French army points out that the transfer of creative energy from Britain to Rome was facilitated through the involvement of "France".

The aspects that did not fulfill their evolutionary potential, i.e., Lear and Gloucester, have departed. Before they departed, however, they had been partially purified. Lear, after going through purifying experiences, was able to meet Cordelia and in this way to erase partially his ignorance. Gloucester went through a similar process of prolonged suffering; then he met Edgar and asked for his forgiveness. Such partial purification of these aspects is important for Britain. Otherwise, residual traces of such impurities would complicate the process in the future. Such experiences are necessary and beneficial to the future stages of the Celtic cycle. (It is important to notice that this particular step of the process was not realized within the Roman cycle at the time of Octavius Caesar; till his last moment Mark Antony remained boastful and arrogant).

Only the constructive aspects remain on the scene at the end of the play, i.e., Edgar, Kent, and Albany. Albany transfers his responsibilities to Kent and Edgar:

> "Friends of my soul, you twain
> Rule in this realm, and the gored state sustain."

However, Kent realizes that his time is limited:

> "I have a journey, sir, shortly to go;
> My master calls me, I must not say no."

Therefore Edgar becomes the leading aspect of Britain. Now, Britain has to wait for another forceful occasion to discharge its partially recovered evolutionary functionality. Such an occasion will be possible only at some time in the future. Shakespeare describes it in "Cymbeline".

3.2 Renewed Reformation in "Cymbeline"

Introduction

"Cymbeline" is the second play of Shakespeare's Celtic trilogy: the play is a sequel to "King Lear". Therefore it is not surprising that the plot of "Cymbeline" bears a striking resemblance to "King Lear". For example, the relationship between Cymbeline and Imogen parallels that of Lear and Cordelia. Events related to Edgar's and Cordelia's experiences in "King Lear" are re-played in the relationship between Posthumus and Imogen in "Cymbeline".

The readers will note that the main characters of "Cymbeline" demonstrate a remarkable ability to avoid the snares planted throughout the plot. This would indicate that Britain at the time of "Cymbeline" has arrived at a higher stage than that presented in pre-Roman "King Lear". The play explains the cause of such a progress.

The plot of "Cymbeline" is loosely based on a tale told by Geoffrey of Monmouth about the actual British ruler Cunobelinus. Cunobelinus was an early Celtic British King who ruled in Britain around the time of Caesar Augustus.

Technical background

Shakespeare's plays are a remarkable illustration of how the recent phase of evolutionary process was implemented in Western Europe. The plays indicate that a recent turn of the evolutionary spiral consisted of several branches, i.e., Roman, Celtic, Bohemian, English, French, and Italian. These various historical entities and geographical areas responded to the process according to their own specific characteristics. Consequently, customized methodologies were implemented in such a way that they could lead to the most effective outcomes.

For example, the evolutionary fiasco of pre-Roman Britain is illustrated in "King Lear". This was followed by the failure of Rome described in the Roman tetralogy. Later on, as indicated in the analysis of the History Plays, an interaction between the French and English branches led to the birth of the English Renaissance. This sequence of evolutionary events points out that, prior to the activation of the English and French branches, a sophisticated intervention was implemented that allowed to overcome the Rome's failure. "Cymbeline" describes the details of that intervention.

Storyline

Imogen, the daughter of King Cymbeline, goes against her father's wishes and marries a young man of meagre means named Posthumus Leonatus. The marriage of Imogen to Posthumus infuriates King Cymbeline because he had arranged for Imogen to marry his uncouth stepson Cloten. Cloten is the son of Cymbeline's second wife. The Queen has managed to deceive Cymbeline into believing that Cloten has royal qualities and is a worthy heir to Cymbeline's title.

King Cymbeline sends Posthumus into exile in Italy. While Posthumus is at Philario's house in Rome he encounters an Italian named Iachimo. Iachimo argues that all women are naturally unchaste, and he makes a wager with Posthumus that he will be able to seduce Imogen. Iachimo travels to Cymbeline's court and, failing in his initial attempt to seduce Imogen, resorts to trickery: he hides in a large chest and has it sent to Imogen's bedchamber. At night, he slips out and steals a bracelet that Posthumus once gave her.

Cloten continues to pursue Imogen, but she rebuffs him harshly. He becomes furious and vows revenge, while she worries over the loss of her bracelet. In the meantime, Iachimo has returned to Italy, and, displaying the stolen bracelet and an intimate knowledge of the details of Imogen's bedchamber, convinces Posthumus that he won the bet. Posthumus, furious at being betrayed by his wife, sends a letter to Britain ordering his servant, Pisanio, to murder Imogen. But Pisanio believes in Imogen's innocence, and he convinces her to disguise herself as a boy and go search for her husband, while he reports to Posthumus that he has killed her.

Imogen becomes lost in the wilds of Wales. She comes upon a cave where Belarius, an unjustly banished nobleman, lives with his two sons, Guiderius and Arviragus. In fact, the two young men are not his sons but Cymbeline's. Belarius has kidnapped them to avenge his banishment, though they themselves are ignorant of their true parentage. Belarius and his adoptive sons welcome Imogen, who is still dressed as a boy.

At that time Cloten appears, having come in pursuit of Imogen. He provokes Guiderius to fight in duel. Cloten is killed by Guiderius. Imogen, feeling ill, drinks a potion the Queen has prepared for her. The draught induces a deep sleep that resembles death. Belarius and his adoptive sons come upon Imogen and, heart-broken, lay her body beside that of the slain Cloten. Awaking after they have left the scene, she mistakes the body of Cloten for that of Posthumus, and she sinks into despair.

In the meantime, a Roman army has invaded Britain, seeking the restoration of a certain tribute that Britain had ceased to pay. The disguised Imogen hires herself out to them as a page.

Posthumus and Iachimo are traveling with the Roman army, but Posthumus switches to the garb of a peasant and fights valiantly for Britain. He believes that his servant has carried out his orders and killed Imogen. The Romans are defeated, thanks to the intervention of Belarius, Guiderius, and Arviragus. After the battle, Posthumus switches back to the Roman side and is taken prisoner by Cymbeline's soldiers. That night, the god Jupiter informs the spirits of Posthumus' dead ancestors that he will take care of their descendant.

The next day, Cymbeline calls the prisoners before him, and the confusion is sorted out. Posthumus and Imogen are reunited, and they forgive Iachimo, who confesses his deception. The identity of Guiderius and Arviragus is revealed, Belarius is forgiven.

As a final gesture, Cymbeline frees the Roman prisoners and even agrees to resume paying the tribute.

Time factor

There is a time when nothing can be done; a time when something can be done; and a time when most things are achievable. It is possible to develop an inner sense that allows discerning each different quality of time. Such an inner sense operates in the Realm, i.e., outside the limitations of our ordinary sensory perception. From the perspective of the Realm that there is no such thing as past, present and future. The past, present and future appear when the Realm is projected onto our ordinary space-time limited perception. In other words, it is possible, at the level of the Realm, to access the future in order to fix the present[3].

Shakespeare is presenting an example of such a past-present-future intervention in "Cymbeline". The action of "Cymbeline" is placed in 1st century Rome and Britain at the time of Caesar Augustus. However, one of the scenes is placed in 16th century Renaissance Rome[4]. It is a scene in which a Frenchman, a Dutchman, and a Spaniard meet at Philario's house in Rome. The Dutchman and the Spaniard are silent through the entire scene. They serve as a "dumb show" that provides the intended historical background. The Frenchman makes the following comment about Posthumus:

> "I have seen him in France: we had very many there could behold the sun with as firm eyes as he."

This comment indicates that Posthumus, before coming to Rome, has traveled through France where "many there could behold the sun with as firm eyes as he". The Frenchman's comment points out

---

[3] Discoveries of modern science have provided some hints supporting the existence of such interactions. Namely, the special theory of relativity implies the possibility of such a relationship between past, present and future.

[4] Similarly to France in "King Lear", 16th century Rome in "Cymbeline" represents an entity that exists in the future. Both, "France" and "Rome" are a symbolic representation of a higher state of mind. Posthumus' journey to Rome is a description of specific meditative experiences.

that, at the time of Posthumus' stay in France, the French branch was already quite advanced. The initiation of the French branch is related to the time of the creation of the chivalric orders in the 12th century. Shakespeare sends Posthumus to France to emphasize the involvement of the French Chivalric Knight into the Celtic cycle.

Then, there is a scene when Posthumus awakens in a prison in Wales and finds on the ground beside him a richly decorated book. This particular episode belongs to the 9th century tradition of the Celtic branch of the modern evolutionary cycle. This scene is a reference to the Book of Kells - the richly decorated manuscript produced by Columban monks closely associated with the Iona Abbey.

The brief shift from 1st century Britain to 16th century Rome and 9th century Wales - is significant. By placing Posthumus in various historical times Shakespeare illustrates how a certain experience in the future may be used to resolve a situation in the present. Namely, certain advanced developmental techniques were first revealed in the Middles Ages. Then they were mastered in Renaissance Italy and France, so they could be applied to the 9th century situation in Wales. Such an intervention is possible, because, as stated earlier, at the level of the Realm there is no such thing as past, present and future. Shakespeare clearly underlines, however, that such an "intervention" requires the presence of either a highly developed individual or super-corporal aspects representing the Realm. It may help to comprehend such past-present-future relationships to recall that Posthumus' travels occur during his banishment. In Shakespeare's vocabulary "banishment" refers to certain meditative experiences associated with the activation of higher states of mind. During the "banishment" the mind is forced out of its routine operation and is opened to new types of experiences.

It should be emphasized that such a past-present-future intervention has to be chosen from the universal design at the level of the Realm. It is in accordance with this design that cultures and societies are often stages where time must pass before an evolutionary impulse is correctly digested and a new idea can be re-injected in order to be effectively implemented. The entire corpus of Shakespeare's plays is an example of the projection of the universal design onto our ordinary sensory perceptions.

Tribute

It is interesting to see how Shakespeare underlines the fact that "Cymbeline" belongs to the corpus of illustrative history, i.e., a series of events that are concocted to point out a meaning connected with the evolutionary process.

Right at the beginning of the play we learn that Posthumus Leonatus' brothers and his father, Sicilius, were fighting Romans at the time of Julius Caesar. It was at that time that an impulse of unitive energy was made available within the Roman evolutionary cycle. In this way Shakespeare points out that, at that time, Britain was exposed to unitive energy. It is this event that marks the forceful occasion that is alluded to at the conclusion of the analysis of "King Lear".

When Sicilius died and his two elder sons were killed in the battle, the youngest son, Posthumus Leonatus, became the sole aspect of Britain that had been exposed to unitive energy. This is further emphasized by his second name Leonatus, which is the initiate name "Birth of a lion". In this way 1st century Britain becomes a secondary layer of Rome. The established developmental link between Rome and Britain is symbolically indicated as the "tribute" that the king of Britain has to pay to Rome. As soon as the audience realizes that "Cymbeline" is about the revival and preservation of this link, then the play's plot becomes easy to understand and follow.

The Queen and her son Cloten are the obvious villains of the play. Therefore, it should not be surprising that these two characters are the most determined opponents of the tribute. This is clearly illustrated in the scene where Cymbeline, the Queen, and Cloten meet with Caius Lucius, the Roman ambassador, who demands the continuation of the tribute that was begun in Julius Caesar's time. Supported by the Queen and Cloten, Cymbeline refuses to pay it, declaring that Britain is an independent isle and will remain so. In this scene, Shakespeare makes Cloten the most adamant adversary of the tribute. Here is Cloten's response to Caius Lucius:

"There be many Caesars,
Ere such another Julius. Britain is
A world by itself; and we will nothing pay
For wearing our own noses."

...

"Come, there's no more tribute to be paid: our
kingdom is stronger than it was at that time; and,
as I said, there is no moe such Caesars: other of
them may have crook'd noses, but to owe such
straight arms, none."

This scene indicates that Cloten represents an ignorant and insensitive aspect of Britain. In this way Shakespeare makes clear that the play is not concerned with ordinary intellectual or emotional matters. The readers may notice that the ultimate objective of Shakespeare' plays is not related to patriotic or nationalistic sentiments.

Britain: 1st century AD

The most important feature of Cymbeline's Britain is the fact that this being is much more harmonious and stable than Rome.

Firstly, exposure to unitive energy awakens true love. The entire Roman cycle was incapable of attaining such an experience. This is symbolically illustrated as Imogen falling in love with Posthumus, a man of meagre means. Imogen represents an impulse of unitive energy that has been withdrawn from Rome and transferred to Britain at the time of Caesar Augustus. This is an example of an implementation when an impulse has been administered from outside the line of its own actualization to revitalize the process elsewhere.

Secondly, it should be noted that in "Cymbeline", aspects of the self faculty, which are symbolically represented by noblemen and servants, are fully aware of the importance of Posthumus and his effect on the entire being. Here is a comment by the First Lord about Posthumus:

> " … is a creature such
> As, to seek through the regions of the earth
> For one his like, there would be something failing
> In him that should compare. I do not think
> So fair an outward and such stuff within
> Endows a man but he."

The third factor that indicates that Britain has arrived at a more advanced stage is the quality of the meditative state that is symbolically represented by the forest near Milford Haven, on the coast in Wales. Within Rome, such a state was represented by the "ruthless forest" at the time of "Titus Andronicus". Imogen compares Milford Haven to "a haven":

> "To this same blessed Milford: and by the way
> Tell me how Wales was made so happy as
> To inherit such a haven."

It should be noted that all critical events, including the play's conclusion, take place in Wales. The forest was initially populated with Belarius who was banished by Cymbeline. He went there with the kidnapped sons of Cymbeline, Guiderius and Arviragus. Guiderius and Arviragus are the current replacements for Tamora's sons, Chiron and Demetrius. The quality of this particular forest is marked by Guiderius' and Arviragus' attraction to Imogen. Their affection to Imogen is in stark contrast to Tamora's sons contempt towards Lavinia in "Titus Andronicus".

The meditative state is activated during the battle between Roman and British forces. Its evolutionary function is symbolically described as the decisive contribution of Belarius, Guiderius and Arviragus to the Britain's victory:

> "These three,
> Three thousand confident, in act as many –
> For three performers are the file when all
> The rest do nothing - with this word 'Stand, stand,'

Accommodated by the place, more charming
With their own nobleness, which could have turn'd
A distaff to a lance."

. . .

"Two boys, an old man twice a boy, a lane,
Preserved the Britons, was the Romans' bane."

The "three thousand confident" is a sustaining impact that is delivered by Belarius, Guiderius and Arviragus during the battle with Romans.

All these factors, i.e., the awakening of true love, the presence of supportive noblemen and servants, and the access to a fully functional inspirational state, make it possible to revivify the Celtic branch at the time of "Cymbeline".

Imperfections

At the beginning of the play, the leading aspects of Britain that are represented by Cymbeline, the Queen and her son, are still opaque to the effects of the evolutionary impulse. This opaqueness leads Cymbeline to banishing Posthumus. In this way Cymbeline demonstrates that he is not able to perceive Posthumus' role. In the following comment Imogen quite precisely summarizes the current state of the leading aspects of Britain:

"A father cruel, and a step-dame false;
A foolish suitor to a wedded lady,
That hath her husband banish'd."

The banishment of Posthumus introduces a certain interference that has not allowed for a complete absorption of the evolutionary impulse. In the play this interference is described as an interruption in passing instructions that would allow Posthumus to solidify his link with Imogen. Imogen complains to Pisanio that she did not have enough time to instruct Posthumus how to maintain the link:

"I did not take my leave of him, but had
Most pretty things to say: ere I could tell him

How I would think on him at certain hours
Such thoughts and such, or I could make him swear
The shes of Italy should not betray
Mine interest and his honour, or have charged him,
At the sixth hour of morn, at noon, at midnight,
To encounter me with orisons, for then
I am in heaven for him; or ere I could
Give him that parting kiss which I had set
Betwixt two charming words, comes in my father
And like the tyrannous breathing of the north
Shakes all our buds from growing."

As the result of this interference, Posthumus has not been able to
fully absorb Imogen's love; neither has Imogen been completely
unveiled by Posthumus' love. This is illustrated in the play as a
gradual erosion of Posthumus's faith in Imogen. This in turn leads
to unearthing their imperfections. Posthumus' main shortcoming is
his lack of trust. Imogen's imperfections are described as her
naivety and unjustified haughtiness.

At first sight, Imogen may appear to be a perfect woman. If one
judges by ordinary intellectual, social, or emotional criteria it is
difficult to find a flaw in her. However, from the point of view of
Imogen's inner essence, there are a couple of flaws that
Shakespeare subtly indicated.

When Imogen see Iachimo for the first time, she right away realizes
that he is not to be trusted:

"Who may this be? Fie!"

However, because of Imogen's naivety, Iachimo is able to gain her
trust later on. This is an indication of Imogen's imperfection. Even
if this imperfection is a tiny one, at this stage of the process it can
lead – as the play illustrates – to a significant disturbance.

Imogen's other imperfection comes to light when she unnecessarily
abuses Cloten by making a comparison between him and
Posthumus' "meanest garment":

"His meanest garment,
That ever hath but clipp'd his body, is dearer
In my respect than all the hairs above thee,
Were they all made such men."

Later on Imogen will have to experience for herself that she is not able to distinguish between Posthumus' garment and Cloten's body. This happens when Imogen awakes in the forest and sees the headless corpse of Cloten dressed in Posthumus' clothes. She immediately assumes that it is Posthumus' dead body:

"A headless man! The garments of Posthumus!
I know the shape of's leg: this is his hand;
His foot Mercurial; his Martial thigh;
The brawns of Hercules."

Stricken with grief, she lays herself atop Cloten's body. It would be difficult to have a more compelling scene to demonstrate Imogen's unjustified hauteur.

All these imperfections are gradually removed during the play.

Techniques

As indicated in the History Plays there is a certain hierarchy that governs the evolutionary process. This hierarchy encompasses both worlds, visible and invisible. An insight into the invisible hierarchy is given in "Cymbeline". Namely, there are some aspects of the invisible agency that are getting involved in the process. At one point – and this is the critical point of the entire play – it is clearly stated that the entire sequence of events has been directed by the invisible forces that operate within the Realm. This happens when Posthumus' dead ancestors plead with Jupiter, the king of the gods, to take pity on their descendant and restore his fortunes. Then Jupiter himself arrives from the heavens, surrounded by thunder and lightning, riding on the back of an eagle. He berates the spirits for troubling him and grudgingly tells them, and the audience, that Posthumus' affairs have been in the care of "the fingers of the powers above" and that Posthumus' trials "well are spent":

"No care of yours it is; you know 'tis ours.
Whom best I love I cross; to make my gift,
The more delay'd, delighted. Be content;
Your low-laid son our godhead will uplift:
His comforts thrive, his trials well are spent.
Our Jovial star reign'd at his birth, and in
Our temple was he married. Rise, and fade.
He shall be lord of lady Imogen,
And happier much by his affliction made.
This tablet lay upon his breast, wherein
Our pleasure his full fortune doth confine."

When all the supernatural creatures depart, Posthumus awakes and finds on the ground beside him the richly decorated book with a written oracle in it:

"A book? O rare one!
Be not, as is our fangled world, a garment
Nobler than that it covers: let thy effects
So follow, to be most unlike our courtiers,
As good as promise."

Posthumus' words "Be not, as is our fangled world, a garment nobler than that it covers" is a reference to the Book of Kells.

It should be mentioned that Posthumus does not understand the process. His inner state allows him, however, to respond constructively to the various situations that have been prearranged for him. The trials have been designed in such a way that they will unearth Posthumus' inner imperfections, which otherwise could remain hidden hindrances and would prevent him from making progress. As the result of these prearranged events, Posthumus' state could be further purified. At the same time the impulse, which is represented by Imogen, could be fully unveiled.

The involvement of Jupiter is needed to exposure Posthumus to advanced techniques that are available in the future. This is why he has to travel to Renaissance Rome. In this was it was possible to overcome the gap that was created by the Roman evolutionary fiasco.

There are four developmental techniques implemented in "Cymbeline", namely "banishment", "modulation of beauty", "induced jealousy", and "controlled rebuke". The readers may note that, previously, only "banishment" and "rebuke" were applied.

Banishment
Only a "reformed" Posthumus could induce Imogen's love. Therefore, the marriage symbolically indicates the completion of Posthumus' reformation. Now Posthumus has to go through the next stage of the process. In Shakespeare's plays this particular stage is described as "banishment". Posthumus is banished from Britain to Rome. The "banishment" corresponds to a transition into an inspirational state. 16th century Renaissance Rome represents such a meditative state.

Modulation of beauty
When Cymbeline accuses Imogen of degrading Britain's throne:

> "Thou took'st a beggar; wouldst have made my throne
> A seat for baseness."

Imogen explains to him the significance of her marriage to Posthumus:

> "No; I rather added
> A lustre to it."

While comparing Posthumus to an "added lustre", Imogen indicates that Posthumus represents a "polished" or purified aspect of the manifest faculty. The above quote provides an important marker. Namely, the current receptor of the evolutionary impulse is Posthumus, a "beggar" and an "outsider". In this way Shakespeare points out that, at that time, certain exceptional members of humanity at-large gained access to advanced developmental techniques.

Cymbeline is incapable of grasping the meaning of Imogen's

explanation. In this context it is interesting to quote the Second Lord's remark about Imogen:

> "She shines not upon fools, lest the
> reflection should hurt her."

The Lord is able to perceive the inner "beauty" that is represented by Imogen. As the result of her meeting with Posthumus, Imogen's inner beauty has been activated. From that moment on Imogen shines her inner beauty on those who are around her. Those, however, whose inner being is corrupted, or "veiled by darkness", would reflect back some deformed *vibes* that could harm her and others. By the same token, those who are only partially ready to absorb such an impulse could be overwhelmed by it, or be "veiled by sheer lights"[5]. Therefore, it is necessary to modulate the intensity of spiritual "beauty". Shakespeare introduces in "Cymbeline" a literary device that he uses to demonstrate such an effect. Namely, a woman disguised as a boy can "modulate" her impact on those around her. Imogen disguises herself as a boy named Fidele:

> "You must forget to be a woman; change
> Command into obedience: fear and niceness -
> The handmaids of all women, or, more truly,
> Woman its pretty self - into a waggish courage:
> Ready in gibes, quick-answer'd, saucy and
> As quarrelous as the weasel; nay, you must
> Forget that rarest treasure of your cheek,
> Exposing it - but, O, the harder heart!
> Alack, no remedy! - to the greedy touch
> Of common-kissing Titan, and forget
> Your laboursome and dainty trims, wherein
> You made great Juno angry."

Several forms of "modulation of beauty" are implemented in Shakespeare's plays to illustrate its application in various developmental situations.

---

[5] "Veiled by darkness" and "veiled by sheer lights" are technical terms used in spiritual teaching.

Induced jealousy

Shakespeare implies in "Cymbeline" that "jealousy" was applied as an element of the developmental methodology. In other words, "jealousy" is used to unearth the imperfections, i.e., the intensity of the jealousy is proportional to the degree of inner impurities.

Jealousy is introduced in a scene that takes place in Renaissance Italy. In this particular scene the distractive element of "jealousy" is borrowed from the Italian branch. Iachimo (Little Iago) is the instrument of such a distractive impact. This instrument of jealousy, in a more vicious form, is also applied by Iago in "Othello" (see Volume 3, Chapter 6).

Controlled rebuke

"Rebuke" is a technical term that refers to an intentionally created situation, regardless of how painful and traumatic it may be, that makes a constructive impact. In this way, a constructive change may be induced. Shakespeare has introduced in "Cymbeline" another literary device that allows for the illustration of rebuke. This particular device is usually injected into a play's plot as the supposed death of a woman who represents an evolutionary impulse. Pisanio explains to Imogen that some villain must have deceived Posthumus into thinking that Imogen has been unfaithful. Then Pisanio persuades Imogen that by counterfeiting her death, they may instil guilt in Posthumus and restore his love for her. Pisanio sends to Posthumus a piece of blood-stained clothing as proof of Imogen's death.

Indeed, Posthumus is overcome with remorse when he receives the bloody handkerchief from Pisanio, apparently a token of Imogen's death:

> "Gods! if you
> Should have ta'en vengeance on my faults, I never
> Had lived to put on this: so had you saved
> The noble Imogen to repent, and struck
> Me, wretch more worth your vengeance. But, alack,
> You snatch some hence for little faults; that's love,
> To have them fall no more: you some permit

To second ills with ills, each elder worse,
And make them dread it, to the doers' thrift.
But Imogen is your own: do your best wills,
And make me blest to obey!"

When Posthumus receives the bloody handkerchief, he experiences a certain spiritual realization that is the prime objective of this particular technique. Several forms of the "bloody handkerchief" appear in other Shakespeare's plays.

Similarly, the villain Iachimo feels his first pangs of remorse when he is captured by Posthumus during the battle in Wales:

"The heaviness and guilt within my bosom
Takes off my manhood: I have belied a lady,
The princess of this country, and the air on't
Revengingly enfeebles me."

Such a form of rebuke, as briefly outlined above, is a trademark of Shakespeare's plays.

Renewal

The overall outcome of the developmental sequence is summarized in a vision that the Soothsayer describes to Caius Lucius before the battle in Wales:

"I saw Jove's bird, the Roman eagle, wing'd
From the spongy south to this part of the west,
There vanish'd in the sunbeams: which portends -
Unless my sins abuse my divination -
Success to the Roman host."

At the end of the play the Soothsayer further refines the interpretation of his vision, namely:

"The fingers of the powers above do tune
The harmony of this peace. The vision
Which I made known to Lucius, ere the stroke

> Of this yet scarce-cold battle, at this instant
> Is full accomplish'd; for the Roman eagle,
> From south to west on wing soaring aloft,
> Lessen'd herself, and in the beams o' the sun
> So vanish'd: which foreshow'd our princely eagle,
> The imperial Caesar, should again unite
> His favour with the radiant Cymbeline,
> Which shines here in the west."

As indicated earlier, the time of "Cymbeline" encompasses the period when an impulse of unitive energy was made available to Rome. Afterwards, it was used to revive the Celtic branch. The "Roman eagle" represents the release of this impulse of unitive energy. It was made available to humanity during the time of Julius Caesar. Then it was gradually deteriorated ("lessen'd herself") till the time when it vanished "in the beams o' the sun". "The beams o' the sun" refers to the 9th century revival of the evolutionary process in "this part of the west". This is further explained in the oracle that Posthumus found in the richly decorated book after having his visionary dream:

> "When as a lion's whelp shall, to himself unknown,
> without seeking find, and be embraced by a piece of
> tender air; and when from a stately cedar shall be
> lopped branches, which, being dead many years,
> shall after revive, be jointed to the old stock and
> freshly grow; then shall Posthumus end his miseries,
> Britain be fortunate and flourish in peace and plenty."

The Soothsayer explains that:

- -"a lion's whelp" represents Posthumus Leonatus;
- -"a piece of tender air" refers to Imogen;
- -"a stately cedar" with revived branches represents Cymbeline's just-found sons.

The oracle also applies to the overall evolutionary process as implemented in Western Europe. The evolutionary transmission chain is compared to a "stately cedar", while its broken links may be described as "lopped branches". "A lion's whelp" indicates a receptor of evolutionary energy. In every Shakespeare play there is a character that represents such an aspect. The moment, when such an aspect is exposed to an impulse of evolutionary energy, may be described as "embraced by a piece of tender air".

At the end of the play, Imogen and Posthumus are reunited and Cymbeline's abducted sons are restored to him. The Romans are defeated but their lives are spared.

It should be noted that Guiderius, the eldest son of Cymbeline, and not Posthumus, is going to inherit the throne of Britain. Guiderius seems to be a sympathetic, honest, and well-intentioned young man. But he is naïve and lacking deeper perception. He has not developed yet the inner capacities necessary to sustain his reign. The spiritual incapacity of Guiderius will be the cause of disruptions in the Celtic branch in the future.

The final scene of "Cymbeline" sets the stage for the events described in "Macbeth". "Macbeth" illustrates the final episode of the Celtic branch.

Conclusion

The conclusion of the play is summarized by Cymbeline's seemingly surprising decision to restore payment of the tribute to Rome. Cymbeline does it despite the fact that his army triumphed after a bloody battle with the Romans. This "gesture" symbolically indicates that the evolutionary link with the "source" has been restored:

> "The imperial Caesar, should again unite
> His favour with the radiant Cymbeline,
> Which shines here in the west."

The restoration of the link is a result of the above-mentioned intervention into the future that has allowed to remedy the present spiritual state of Britain.

Both, Britain and Rome, faced the same challenge of

accommodating creative energy. As illustrated in "King Lear" and "Titus Andronicus", the impulse had to be withdrawn. At the time of Caesar Octavius, however, the developmental state of Britain was more stable and more balanced than Rome's. This is why it was possible for Britain to overreach all the way towards unitive energy. This more steady state of Britain was achieved through the corrective action implemented at the end of "King Lear". Despite the apparently tragic ending of King Lear, the corrupted aspects were effectively eliminated. King Lear went through a series of difficult trials and was able to erase partially his ignorance. Some 10 centuries later this experience allowed Lear's successor, i.e., Cymbeline, to overcome his own mistakes.

Because of its familiarity with the universal design and the evolutionary patterns, the Celtic initiate system gained access to advanced techniques in the 9th century AD, i.e., earlier than other parts of Western Europe. In this way the Celtic initiate system served as a vehicle for bringing the advanced techniques to Europe.

Wes Jamroz

3.3 Conjugate Cycle in "Macbeth"

Introduction

"Macbeth", like all Shakespeare's plays, is an illustration of a part of the evolutionary process. Therefore, labelling this play as a "tragedy" applies only to its emotional or external content. Dividing Shakespeare's plays into "tragedies" and "comedies" diminishes their inner content. Such classification makes it very difficult, or even impossible, for the readers to discern the inner narrative of the plays. It is a process that is described in these plays. This process includes many experiences, which sometimes may seem comical, sometimes may be perceived as tragic. Nevertheless, all these experiences have to be encountered and they are unavoidable. Each of these experiences is a preparation for other ones; in all cases they lead to a constructive outcome.

Technical background

A diminishing cycle refers to a case when a person, a country, or an entire culture has not been able, for whatever reason, to sustain the previously absorbed evolutionary energy. In such a case, the being goes through situations that repeat themselves, one after another. This may be symbolically illustrated as an unstable kingdom. At the beginning there may be a good and honest king. He may be a virtuous and benevolent ruler. However, he does not have enough skills, strength, support and capacity to protect and sustain his kingdom. As the result, he is either killed or overpowered by a wicked and more aggressive aspect. This is followed by confusion, chaos, destruction, and tyranny. In turn, this usually leads to a short-lived rebellion of the masses. Then another king is brought on the scene. He is in power for a while, but he is not able to sustain the order either. And these situations repeat over and over again. Such sequences of events are examples of what is called a vicious circle. If there were no influx of evolutionary energies at all, then each time, such a kingdom would be falling to a lower and lower level of its evolutionary potential. Its evolutionary entropy would be increasing. After some time such a kingdom would gradually diminish to the point of no return. As illustrated in "King Lear" and "Cymbeline", such a situation can be avoided through the activation of a secondary layer.

"Macbeth" illustrates a slightly different variant of the protective mechanism. Namely, the protective mechanism takes the form of a natural "source" of evolutionary energy. For example, there are certain individuals who are born with a natural goodness. This lifts them to a level which for most people is obtainable only with the greatest efforts. They are loyal, gentle and unselfish souls that are endowed with a natural intuition for good and a natural inclination to pursue it. Their function is to comfort and stabilize those who are fortunate enough to be in their presence.

It is important to underline the fact that such natural sources are not capable of bringing a being onto a higher stage of development. However, they may protect against evolutionary extinction. "Macbeth" illustrates the operation of such a natural source.

Storyline

At the beginning of the play, the Scottish King Duncan hears the news that his generals, Macbeth and Banquo, have defeated two separate invading armies from the Western Isles and Norway. Following their battle with these enemy forces, Macbeth and Banquo encounter three witches. The witches prophesy that Macbeth will become thane of Cawdor and then king of Scotland. The witches also prophesy that Macbeth's friend, Banquo, will never be king himself but will beget a line of Scottish kings. Macbeth and Banquo are sceptical about the prophecy. Then they meet some of King Duncan's men who come to tell Macbeth that he has indeed been named thane of Cawdor. Macbeth is awestruck by the possibility that the second part of the witches' prophecy might also be true.

King Duncan invites himself to dine with Macbeth and his wife at their castle. When Lady Macbeth learns from her husband about the witches' prophecy, she wants Macbeth to become king. She manages to override her husband's objections and persuades him to kill King Duncan that very night. Macbeth murders Duncan and seizes the throne for himself. Duncan's son Malcolm flees to England, fearing that whoever killed Duncan desires his death as well.

Macbeth, fearful of the witches' other part of the prophecy that Banquo's heirs will inherit the throne, hires murderers to kill Banquo and his son Fleance. The murderers kill Banquo, but Fleance escapes. At the feast that night Banquo's ghost appears to Macbeth. When he sees the ghost, Macbeth becomes delirious and his behaviour frightens his guests.

Afterwards Macbeth decides to see the witches again. The witches warn him that he must beware of Macduff, a Scottish nobleman who opposed Macbeth's accession to the throne. Then the witches present him with further prophecies. They tell Macbeth that any man born of woman cannot harm him and that he will be safe until Birnam Wood comes to Dunsinane Castle. Macbeth is relieved and feels secure because he knows that all men are born of women and forests cannot move. When he learns that Macduff has fled to England to join Malcolm, Macbeth orders that Macduff's castle be seized and that his wife and his children be murdered. Macduff is stricken with grief when he learns about his family's execution. He vows revenge.

In the meantime, Malcolm, Duncan's son, is looking for the support of the English king. His invasion plans have the support of the Scottish nobles who are frightened by Macbeth's tyrannical and murderous behaviour.

Before Macbeth's opponents arrive, Macbeth receives news that Lady Macbeth has killed herself. Then Macbeth learns that Malcolm's army is advancing on Dunsinane shielded with boughs cut from Birnam Wood. In other words, Birnam Wood is indeed coming to Dunsinane, fulfilling half of the witches' prophecy. Macbeth is struck with fear.

In the battle, Macbeth fights fiercely, but Malcolm's forces gradually overwhelm his army and castle. On the battlefield, Macbeth encounters the vengeful Macduff, who declares that he was not of woman born but was instead "untimely ripped" from his mother's womb, i.e., his birth was by Caesarean section. Macbeth continues to fight until Macduff kills and beheads him.

Malcolm becomes the king of Scotland.

Parallel transmissions

A brief historical note may provide additional details that can help to understand the play.

Shakespeare's plays indicate that, historically, the effects of the activation of the modern evolutionary cycle reached various parts of Europe at different times. For example, England was exposed to it at the time of Geoffrey the Fair, Duke of Anjou (1113 - 1151). This exposure allowed to form the English branch of the modern cycle.

Shakespeare has placed the action of "Macbeth" prior to that time, i.e., before the English branch was activated. Namely, Shakespeare's Macbeth represents the historical figure of Mac Bethad mac Findlaích. This Mac Bethad was King of Scots from 1040 until his death in 1057. He is buried in Iona Abbey.

The play "Macbeth" is an illustration of the conjugate interaction between the Celtic and English branches of the modern evolutionary cycle.

Scotland: 11th century AD

As indicated previously, the sophistication and characteristics of the destructive agents correspond to the spiritual state of the being. The more advanced the being, the more sophisticated are the invisible forces and attractions that are attached to it and conjugated with it. And the opposite is also true. The more degenerate a being, the more primitive and simplistic are the invisible forces attached to it. This is clearly illustrated in "Macbeth". The being of Scotland is weak and unstable; it can be easily put out of balance. Therefore, this being is an easy target for simplistic destructive forces.

King Duncan, his son Malcolm, Macbeth, Lady Macbeth, Banquo, and Macduff are the leading aspects. Duncan, Malcolm, and Banquo represent aspects of the intellect faculty. Macbeth, Lady Macbeth, and Macduff illustrate aspects of the heart faculty.

At the beginning of the play, Scotland is led by King Duncan. Duncan is a virtuous and benevolent ruler. However, he does not have the inner capacities needed to sustain his reign. He is rather naïve and lacks deeper perception.

Macbeth and Lady Macbeth represent the corrupted aspects. They both are greedy and corruptible. Macbeth is a brave general but he is not virtuous. Lady Macbeth is an ambitious woman who desires power and position. Her comment about her baby clearly marks her determination and her persuasive skills:

> "I have given suck, and know
> How tender 'tis to love the babe that milks me:
> I would, while it was smiling in my face,
> Have pluck'd my nipple from his boneless gums,
> And dash'd the brains out, had I so sworn as you
> Have done to this."

The most noticeable feature of Scotland is the absence of an impulse of unitive energy. The readers will recall that such an impulse was transferred from Rome to the Celtic branch at the time of "Cymbeline". In the 9th century AD this impulse greatly influenced the Celtic branch. At the time of "Macbeth", however, this impulse is not present. The above comment by Lady Macbeth about her dead baby is a symbolic indication that unitive energy was withdrawn from the Celtic branch sometime between the 9th and the 11th century AD. The impulse of unitive energy was deactivated and stored somewhere in Western Europe.

Banquo represents the most conscious and advanced aspect of

Scotland. He is the current link to the evolutionary transmission chain. However, he is incapable of influencing other aspects of this being. His role is limited to giving advice to Macbeth and warning others. King Duncan is incapable of recognizing Banquo's functionality. In his naivety, King Duncan treats Macbeth and Banquo equally. Therefore, Duncan is not able to keep his throne for long.

Banquo's perception is demonstrated right at the beginning of the play, when he and Macbeth encounter the witches. The witches promise Banquo that his descendants will inherit the Scottish throne:

> First Witch:
> "Lesser than Macbeth, and greater."
> Second Witch:
> "Not so happy, yet much happier."
> Third Witch:
> "Thou shalt get kings, though thou be none:
> So all hail, Macbeth and Banquo!"

Unlike Macbeth, Banquo does not translate the witches' prophecy into action. He does not allow himself to fall into the witches' trap. Banquo perceives the role of the destructive agents. He tries to explain it to Macbeth:

> "And oftentimes, to win us to our harm,
> The instruments of darkness tell us truths,
> Win us with honest trifles, to betray's
> In deepest consequence."

Macbeth, following the witches' prophecy, sees Banquo as a threat to his desire for power. He orders that Banquo be murdered. Afterwards Banquo's ghost silently rebukes Macbeth's actions. In this way this ghostly aspect tries again to protect Macbeth against the witches' trap. At the same time the ghost warns Macbeth's guests about their host's madness. And that is the limit of how far this ghostly aspect is able to influence the current situation. The ghost is not able to counter the destructive tendencies that have been unearthed by the witches' prophecies. Macbeth ignores all the warnings. He chooses a path that leads him to his gradual degeneration.

According to the motto, "like attracts like", the destructive forces attached to Scotland are not perfect in their actions either. Hecate, the goddess of witchcraft, is upset at the witches because they have not consulted with her before their first encounter with Macbeth. Hecate is angry because the witches invested their charms in a rather weak aspect of Scotland. From Hecate's perspective, Macbeth is not vicious enough. He is not able to serve evil efficiently enough. Macbeth is only after his own personal greed and simplistic wants:

> "Have I not reason, beldams as you are,
> Saucy and overbold? How did you dare
> To trade and traffic with Macbeth
> In riddles and affairs of death;
> And I, the mistress of your charms,
> The close contriver of all harms,
> Was never call'd to bear my part,
> Or show the glory of our art?
> And, which is worse, all you have done
> Hath been but for a wayward son,
> Spiteful and wrathful, who, as others do,
> Loves for his own ends, not for you."

Macbeth can be easily corrupted. However, he is not truly a villain to the extent that, for example, Aaron is in "Titus Andronicus". Macbeth does not represent the same degree of viciousness and determination. As a matter of fact, he is rather weak and shaky in handling himself. Hecate is upset because of the effect that the ghost of Banquo has had on Macbeth. Macbeth has been completely distracted by the appearance of the ghost. Macbeth's "loves for his own ends, not for you" may spoil Hecate's overall objective. Therefore, she has to implement a contingency plan. Hecate tells the witches that when Macbeth comes the next time they must summon visions and spirits whose messages will enhance Macbeth's viciousness by filling him with a false sense of security and drawing him into a stronger determination towards his wicked quest:

"And that distill'd by magic sleights
Shall raise such artificial sprites
As by the strength of their illusion
Shall draw him on to his confusion:
He shall spurn fate, scorn death, and bear
He hopes 'bove wisdom, grace and fear:
And you all know, security
Is mortals' chiefest enemy."

At the end of his second encounter with the witches, Macbeth is shown a procession of eight crowned kings, the last carrying a mirror. Banquo's ghost walks at the end of the line. Here is Macbeth's reaction to this vision:

"Thou art too like the spirit of Banquo: down!
Thy crown does sear mine eye-balls. And thy hair,
Thou other gold-bound brow, is like the first.
A third is like the former. Filthy hags!
Why do you show me this? A fourth! Start, eyes!
What, will the line stretch out to the crack of doom?
Another yet! A seventh! I'll see no more:
And yet the eighth appears, who bears a glass
Which shows me many more; and some I see
That two-fold balls and treble scepters carry:
Horrible sight! Now, I see, 'tis true;
For the blood-bolter'd Banquo smiles upon me,
And points at them for his."

The procession of kings enhances Macbeth's craving to father a line of kings. Macbeth demands to know the meaning of this final vision, but the witches perform a dance and then they withdraw.

It is obvious that the witches' prophecies are constructed in such a way that they would affect the hearer according to this hearer's inner state. It is in this manner that the prophecies may become self-fulfilling. The audience can clearly see how Macbeth has been influenced by these simplistic messages. On the other hand, however, the witches' prophecies have to be based on a template that consists of an accurate presentation of future events. Their means are limited to a marginal degree of deceptive emphasis and biased presentation. It is interesting to see how Shakespeare uses the witches to describe an effect that is technically known as "the mischief of the whisperer who withdraws after his whispering".

Macduff's mission

The most difficult role in the process that is described in "Macbeth" has been given to Macduff.

Macduff is a Scottish nobleman who is hostile to Macbeth's kingship from the very beginning. His role may be easily misunderstood because it goes against ordinary norms of social and family conventions. Macduff intuitively follows his "heart desire", without being able to comprehend its overall implications. His heart desire, however, is not driven by ordinary love. In order to discharge his mission, Macduff has to flee Scotland and leave behind his wife and children. No ordinary human norms would accept such an action. No wonder that Lady Macduff feels betrayed and demands an explanation as to why her husband has fled to England and left her alone with the children. When she is told that she should trust her husband's wisdom, she cannot accept that:

> "Wisdom! to leave his wife, to leave his babes,
> His mansion and his titles in a place
> From whence himself does fly? He loves us not;
> He wants the natural touch: for the poor wren,
> The most diminutive of birds, will fight,
> Her young ones in her nest, against the owl.
> All is the fear and nothing is the love;
> As little is the wisdom, where the flight
> So runs against all reason."

At this stage of the development it is beyond Lady Macduff's ability to comprehend her husband's actions.

Macduff joins Malcolm's forces in England. At the beginning of their encounter, Malcolm does not trust him either, because

173

Macduff abandoned his wife and children. Therefore, Malcolm suspects that Macduff may be secretly working for Macbeth. While talking with Macduff, Malcolm rambles on about his own vices. In this way he tries to determine from Macduff's reaction whether he is trustworthy. Macduff passes Malcolm's test of loyalty. Macduff becomes the leader of the campaign to unseat Macbeth. The campaign's goal is to place Malcolm on the throne.

However, there is still a very important requirement that has to be fulfilled before such a mission can be accomplished.

Protective source

As has been mentioned earlier, there are natural sources that may protect man against his evolutionary extinction. Such a protective role at the time of "Macbeth" has been bestowed upon King Edward of England. Without the activation of a link with this "source" it would be impossible to restore the balance of Scotland:

> "The son of Duncan,
> From whom this tyrant holds the due of birth
> Lives in the English court, and is received
> Of the most pious Edward with such grace
> That the malevolence of fortune nothing
> Takes from his high respect: thither Macduff
> Is gone to pray the holy king, upon his aid."

Shakespeare describes King Edward as a miracle maker and a natural healer. This is illustrated in a scene that takes place outside King Edward's palace. A doctor appears briefly and says that a "crew of wretched souls" is waiting for King Edward so they may be cured:

> "Ay, sir; there are a crew of wretched souls
> That stay his cure: their malady convinces
> The great assay of art; but at his touch-
> Such sanctity hath heaven given his hand-
> They presently amend."

When the doctor leaves, Macduff asks:

"What's the disease he means?"

Malcolm explains that King Edward has a miraculous power to cure disease "called the evil":

" 'Tis call'd the evil:
A most miraculous work in this good king;
Which often, since my here-remain in England,
I have seen him do. How he solicits heaven,
Himself best knows: but strangely-visited people,
All swoln and ulcerous, pitiful to the eye,
The mere despair of surgery, he cures,
Hanging a golden stamp about their necks,
Put on with holy prayers: and 'tis spoken,
To the succeeding royalty he leaves
The healing benediction. With this strange virtue,
He hath a heavenly gift of prophecy,
And sundry blessings hang about his throne,
That speak him full of grace."

Shakespeare uses the historical figure of King Edward the Confessor to illustrate the working of the protective mechanism. King Edward represents a natural repository of spiritual energy[6].

It should be emphasized that Macduff, not Malcolm, activates the link between Scotland and King Edward. This is Macduff's pivotal role. His mission is to secure the potential for the future evolutionary uplifting of Scotland. Macduff is provided with King Edward's "ten thousand English soldiers". This is the most critical moment of the entire process described in "Macbeth". The "ten thousand English soldiers" symbolically illustrate a sustaining impulse provided by King Edward.

---

[6] King Edward the Confessor was the penultimate Anglo-Saxon King of England, from 1042 until his death in 1066. After the reign of Henry II of England (1154 - 1189), Saint Edward the Confessor was considered the patron saint of England. However, during the reign of King Edward III, i.e., since the "initiation" and the formation of the Order of the Garter in 1348, Saint George became the patron saint of the English monarchy.

In this context it is interesting to note that Birnam Wood in "Macbeth" symbolically represents an inspirational state. Birnam Wood with "ten thousand English soldiers" comes to Macbeth's Dunsinane Castle. It is there that Macduff kills Macbeth. Malcolm becomes king of Scotland.

Shakespeare's Celtic trilogy describes a series of experiences associated with the inspirational state. This meditative state is symbolically illustrated as (i) a simple hut on a heath in "King Lear"; (ii) a forest near Milford Haven in "Cymbeline"; and (iii) Birnam Wood in "Macbeth". It is there that the leading characters are banished to. The hut on the heath is used to activate the secondary layer. The forest near Milford Haven allows to revivify the Celtic evolutionary branch. Macbeth is killed when he, Malcolm, and Macduff are "banished" to Birnam Wood.

Shakespeare uses unique tracers to help the readers link together certain plays into the corresponding evolutionary branches. For example, the characters "untimely born" are such a tracer for the Celtic trilogy. In "King Lear" Edmund "came something saucily into the world before he was sent for"; Posthumus' mother in "Cymbeline" reveals that "from me was Posthumus ript"; and "Macduff was from his mother's womb untimely ripp'd" in "Macbeth". The untimely birth is a symbolic representation of the inopportune release of evolutionary energy that strongly affected the Celtic branch.

Conjugate cycle

All of the witches' predictions, including the prophecy about Banquo's heirs, are fulfilled either within the course of "Macbeth" or they are described in other Shakespeare's plays. Shakespeare indicates that Fleance, Banquo's son, survives Macbeth's attempt to murder him. At the end of the play, however, Fleance's whereabouts are unknown. This is an indicator that the link to the evolutionary transmission chain has been preserved.

It is quite remarkable how Shakespeare has linked "Macbeth" to the History Plays. This link is indicated in the witches' image of the procession of kings. The seven "kings" who form the procession parallel the seven evolutionary stages that are described in the History Plays. The kings are linked together; their common feature is "golden" hair, i.e., the sign of their spiritual initiation. Of course, the last one, i.e., the eighth king who carries a mirror, corresponds to Elizabeth I in "Henry VIII". In symbolic language, a polished "mirror" represents a purified aspect of the manifest faculty. This is a direct reference to the stage symbolically represented by Elizabeth I at the end of "Henry VIII".

The seven "kings" are descendants of Banquo in the sense that they represent a latent transmission chain that links Scotland at the time of "Macbeth" with England at the time of "Henry VIII". It was at the time of Elizabeth I, and James I, that the next forceful occasion occurred. It was then that these two branches of the modern evolutionary cycle, the Celtic and the English, were united.

Macbeth sees in the mirror reflections of many "developed" men. Some of those men carry two balls and three sceptres that indicate that they are kings of more than one "country". These "kings" correspond to post-Elizabethan spiritual descendants of Banquo. Ironically, this image which is most horrifying to Macbeth carries in itself the most promising message for Scotland. Indeed, the procession of kings emphasizes the constructive outcome of the events described in "Macbeth": the spiritual lineage that the witches have indicated to Banquo:

> "Lesser than Macbeth, and greater."
> "Not so happy, yet much happier."
> "Thou shalt get kings, though thou be none."

At this point it should be noted that King James I, Shakespeare's patron, claimed descent from the historical character of Banquo. James was King of Scots as James VI, and King of England and King of Ireland as James I. King James I, sitting on the throne at Shakespeare's time, was separated from the historical Banquo by nine generations.

The Celtic branch was revivified as the result of exposure to unitive energy. This branch, however, was lacking creative energy. Without creative energy, the Celtic inner structure was not complete. Therefore it could not be sustained. This means that the Celtic branch could only be used as a temporary repository of unitive energy. As illustrated in "Macbeth", by the 11th century AD the impulse of unitive energy was deactivated and it was stored somewhere in Western Europe. According to Shakespeare's presentation, this particular impulse was re-activated within the Italian branch in the 14th century AD (see Volume 3, Chapter 6).

Conclusion

Malcolm's restoration to the throne signals the return of Scotland to its previous balance. Malcolm's restoration, however, is not of the same quality as, for example, the coronation of Richmond at the conclusion of "Richard III" in the History Plays. Scotland's spiritual state has not been uplifted. But it has been protected against spiritual extinction.

The procession of kings in "Macbeth" is another indication that the release of Shakespeare's plays during the reigns of Elizabeth I and James I was an "announcement" to the world that a certain evolutionary cycle of Western European society had been completed.

Wes Jamroz

www.ingramcontent.com/pod-product-compliance
Lightning Source LLC
LaVergne TN
LVHW021447080426
835509LV00018B/2193